UNLIKELY
ENTREPRENEURS

UNLIKELY
ENTREPRENEURS

WINS, LOSSES, AND CRUCIAL LESSONS ON
BUILDING GREAT COMPANIES

N. LOUIS SHIPLEY • PATRICIA FAVREAU

WILEY

For general information on our other products and services or for technical support, please contact our Customer Care Department within the United States at (800) 762-2974, outside the United States at (317) 572-3993 or fax (317) 572-4002.

Wiley also publishes its books in a variety of electronic formats. Some content that appears in print may not be available in electronic formats. For more information about Wiley products, visit our web site at www.wiley.com.

Library of Congress Cataloging-in-Publication Data is Available:

ISBN: 978-1-394-34589-2 (Cloth)
ISBN: 978-1-394-34590-8 (ePub)
ISBN: 978-1-394-34591-5 (ePDF)

Cover Design: Wiley
Cover Image: © Yutthana Gaetgeaw/Getty Images
Author Photos: Evgenia Eliseeva & Priscilla Fitzgerald, Ambrose Photography

Printed and bound by CPI Group (UK) Ltd, Croydon, CR0 4YY

C9781394345892_101225

We dedicate this book to the entrepreneurs—unlikely or otherwise—who are building the future.

Contents

About the Authors

Evgenia Eliseeva & Priscilla Fitzgerald, Ambrose Photography

Over the combined 20 years that **N. Louis "Lou" Shipley** has taught in the entrepreneurship units at Harvard Business School and MIT Sloan School of Management, he's mentored and advised thousands of MBAs and alumni on how to sell their start-ups' products and how best to scale and grow their companies. He is the former CEO of Black Duck Software, Turbonomic, and Reflectent Software and has experienced entrepreneurship from multiple perspectives: start-up employee, sales leader, manager, investor, advisor, and board member. In 2023, he co-founded the Trinity College Entrepreneurship Center. His articles have been published in *Harvard Business Review* and The *Wall Street Journal*. He lives in Andover, Massachusetts, with his wife and three children.

Evgenia Eliseeva & Priscilla Fitzgerald, Ambrose Photography

For the past two decades **Patricia Favreau** has worked in the Media Relations Department at the MIT Sloan School of Management where she dissects complex academic research for business audiences around the globe. Among her responsibilities, she regularly promotes MBA start-ups and entrepreneurial initiatives. Prior to MIT Sloan, she served as a senior publicist at WGBH Channel 2 Boston. She began her career as a news correspondent for the *Sentinel & Enterprise* and the *Worcester Telegram & Gazette* where she wrote her earliest entrepreneur profiles. She lives in the Boston area with her husband, daughter, and a mischievous pet whippet.

Introduction

You have a great idea for a company, but a fear of failure, little entrepreneurial exposure, or a lack of access to capital is holding you back from exploring the possibilities.

The thought of launching your own company excites you, but between family commitments and other responsibilities, it doesn't seem feasible.

You've launched a start-up but are struggling to keep it afloat.

Your start-up is doing well, but you are unsure how to scale and expand your offerings.

If you see yourself in any of these scenarios, you're not alone. In *Unlikely Entrepreneurs: Wins, Losses, and Crucial Advice on Building Great Companies*, we profile successful entrepreneurs from across the socioeconomic spectrum and multiple industries, many of whom faced fears or doubts about launching their company. All encountered challenges at different points of their entrepreneurial journey. Here are just some of the entrepreneurs you will meet and learn from:

Matthew Riley, O2 Daisy: A former typewriter and fax repairman who left school at 16, Matthew launched Daisy Group—one of the U.K.'s largest independent business-to-business unified communications companies—from a desk in his garage. Following a merger with Virgin Media O2 in August

2025, their new company, O2 Daisy—which Matthew chairs—is valued at more than $3 billion.[1]

Bill Warner, Avid Technology: Breaking his back in a car accident as a teenager gave Bill permission to follow his heart, a journey that resulted in the creation of Avid Media Composer. By 2000, more than 100 television shows and movies were edited using his pioneering digital nonlinear film and video editing system including Hollywood blockbusters like *Titanic* and *The Matrix*, and today it remains the industry standard. The impact of Media Composer has been honored with a Grammy, 16 Emmys, and two Oscars.[2]

Katie Couric, Katie Couric Media: Upon reaching a crossroads in her career, the award-winning broadcast journalist and her husband John Molner launched Katie Couric Media, a fast growing, diversified digital media company in a crowded, increasingly fractured, and highly competitive media market.

Scott Ginsberg, Titan Casket: Described in his youth as a "ship without a rudder," Scott founded Titan Casket, the largest online, direct-to-consumer seller of caskets and funeral products in the United States. In 2025, *Ad Age* named Titan Casket to its Marketers to Watch list "following a year of innovative and edgy marketing campaigns that have garnered attention and solidified Titan Casket's position as a disruptive force in the funeral industry.[3]" Pop legend Taylor Swift peeked out of a Titan casket in her music video *Anti-Hero*.

Cara Nicoletti, Seemore Meats & Veggies: A butcher who majored in literature and philosophy, Cara's innovative approach to creating a healthier sausage stuffed with vegetables produced profits for her employers but not for her. Recognizing a receptive market, she went on to face many challenges in building her start-up whose launch coincided with the start of the COVID-19 lockdown. But she persevered, and today Seemore Meats & Veggies is distributed nationally.

Among the 17 entrepreneurs we've interviewed, some grew up working class or surrounded by poverty. Others had access to opportunities and resources. Regardless of their background, our entrepreneurs have this in common: they possessed a solid business idea big enough to build a company that lasts.

Insights Gleaned from a Harvard Business School (HBS) Classroom and MIT Sloan School of Management Academic Research and Experts: In our respective roles, we have the privilege of working with some of the world's most promising MBA students at HBS and MIT Sloan. Over the combined 20 years that Lou has taught in the entrepreneurship units at HBS and MIT Sloan, he's mentored and advised thousands of MBAs and alumni on how to sell their start-ups' products and how best to scale and grow their companies. In *Unlikely Entrepreneurs*, he brings readers into his HBS classroom and shares those lessons. Lou has experienced entrepreneurship from multiple perspectives: three-time software company CEO, start-up employee, sales leader, manager, and, now, investor advisor and board member. He currently serves on four software boards and is a trustee at Trinity College. In 2023, he co-founded the Trinity College Entrepreneurship Center. Lou kicked off his long career in sales as a teenager when he sold books door-to-door to finance his college education.

Patricia Favreau is a longtime publicist with the Media Relations Department at the MIT Sloan School of Management, who, for more than two decades, has dissected complex academic research for global business audiences. She regularly publicizes MBA start-ups, entrepreneurship competition winners, and faculty authored books—including the best-selling *Disciplined Entrepreneurship: 24 Steps to a Successful Startup* by MIT Sloan Professor of the Practice Bill Aulet. She wrote her first entrepreneur profiles during her college years while working as a news correspondent for the *Sentinel & Enterprise* and the *Worcester Telegram & Gazette*.

Our Book's Origin Story

Patricia believed entrepreneurship could have been her father's salvation. A brilliant inventor who never finished high school, he modified and improved upon the tools he used as an auto mechanic. But her father had never sought patents. When Patricia was young, she remembers him reading in a local newspaper about an entrepreneur who launched a company selling specially designed tools. "I've created tools like that," he said as he quietly folded the newspaper before heading out to his weekend job pumping gas at a nearby station.

Through her work at MIT Sloan, Patricia was inspired to flesh out her own business idea, write a business plan, and create a logo. But she lacked confidence in pursuing entrepreneurship. Much like her father's experience, she'd later read about a startup with an idea similar to her own. Unlike her father, she was frustrated with herself. She reasoned that there had to be entrepreneurs out there who lacked entrepreneurial know-how or faced personal challenges but had nevertheless taken the plunge. She wanted to learn from them what it took to succeed.

Patricia reached out to Lou in 2022 for feedback on a book idea she had on unlikely entrepreneurs. She'd worked with him at MIT Sloan on writing and placing an opinion piece in a business publication and valued his entrepreneurial background. It turned out he knew several unlikely entrepreneurs from his many roles including working at six start-ups and running three. Together, they wrote a case study on a start-up led by an unlikely entrepreneur that was published by HBS. They knew they were on to something.

How Our Book Is Organized

In *Unlikely Entrepreneurs*, we combine elements of the case study method with engaging storytelling that introduces readers to real people and real personal and business dilemmas. We explore key challenges that founders face and the results of their decisions.

Unlikely Entrepreneurs is built around seven topics that entrepreneurs must master to succeed. We incorporate expert insights from MIT Sloan and HBS academics, venture capitalists, investors, founders and CEOs, among others, who offer advice from their unique perspectives.

Chapter 1
The Problem with the "Problem": *Is Your Idea Big Enough to Start a Business That Will Last?*

Too many entrepreneurs mistakenly assume their new product or service will drive demand. Instead, entrepreneurs must ask themselves: would their target market agree the product solves a major problem—a 10 on a scale of 1 to 10—that they're struggling with? This chapter reveals how to gain crucial second-hand knowledge of your target audience's needs and how to build a go-to-market playbook based on methods Lou teaches at HBS.

Chapter 2
Delegate Sales at Your Own Peril: *Why Founders Must Become the Chief Salesperson*

If you are uncomfortable with sales or choose to delegate selling your start-up's product or service, you may find yourself struggling to hire and manage an effective sales team. But to master selling, you must first tackle any underlying disdain for or misconceptions about sales that you may be harboring. In this chapter, Lou takes readers into his entrepreneurial sales course and unpacks the keys to successful selling.

Chapter 3
Fundraising: *It's Like Sales. Except It Isn't*

This chapter explores best practices in working with those helping to fund your business and includes how to avoid "Oops, I lost your money" conversations with family and friends, courting venture capitalists, and what angel investors need from you. We also debunk common myths behind launching and running a nonprofit.

Chapter 4
Leadership: *The Sled Only Moves as Fast as the Lead Dog*

Don't pay employees to work hard—pay them to win. In this chapter, we share start-up hiring best practices and what it takes to build and lead winning teams along with leadership challenges inherent in entrepreneurship through acquisition (ETA).

Chapter 5
Marketing and Promotional Campaigns: *They're More Than Just a Megaphone*

Many entrepreneurs don't build a marketing campaign until after their business is launched. This is a mistake. In this chapter, we examine how to incorporate your marketing efforts into the very beginning of the product's evolution. We take a deep dive into understanding how reporters think, how to pitch stories, media training essentials, social media and digital marketing best practices, and how to leverage AI to build your promotional campaigns.

Chapter 6
Reframing Failure: *The Art of the Pivot*

Many, if not all, start-ups pivot at some point to reinvent their business. This chapter delves into knowing when and how to pivot and what it takes to protect your company or save it from failure. Sometimes it may mean a founder must be willing to kill the idea they love.

Chapter 7
Endings and Beginnings
This chapter busts the myth that entrepreneurship has an age limit and sheds light on how, when, and why entrepreneurs should sell their companies and how to maximize returns. We also explore creating a legacy.

We live in a time of rapid change. The spirit of entrepreneurial innovation and new, daring start-ups are needed more now than ever before to tackle problems both big and small. Our unlikely entrepreneurs and experts will help show you what it takes to succeed.

1

The Problem with "The Problem"

Is Your Idea Big Enough to Start a Business That Will Last?

1.1 Living the Problem: Why Firsthand Experience Matters

The success or failure of all ventures hinges on this: the depth of your relationship with the problem you aim to solve. If you identify the wrong problem, you may persevere in meeting your goals, but you will still fail in the long run.

Over the combined 20 years that Lou has taught in the entrepreneurship units at Harvard Business School (HBS) and MIT Sloan School of Management, he's been approached by hundreds of students and alumni asking for advice on how best to sell their start-ups' product or service. These students and alumni are smart, ambitious, and determined to succeed. But as Lou asked questions, it's not uncommon for him to discover that their business ideas weren't born out of any real experience with the problems they've envisioned solving. In particular, those with new technology products have often believed they've created a whole new market to solve problems consumers don't yet realize they have.

These students and alumni—like many new to entrepreneurship or those looking to expand their company's offerings— mistakenly assume their product or service will drive public demand. This mindset also has its fingerprints on failed companies from across hyped technology cycles—the cloud, blockchain, crypto currency, and, now, machine learning and artificial intelligence. We refer to this as technology in search of a solution.

When Lou has asked how many people the students and alums have spoken with who are struggling with the problem their product aims to solve, he's often met with a quizzical look. Sometimes conversations with a few colleagues or friends are mentioned. But it boils down to this: they've spent so much time envisioning a new, cutting-edge product or service that they haven't asked two crucial questions: does your target market agree that your product or service solves a major problem they're currently struggling with? And is this problem bigger than other problems they face—on a scale of 1 to 10, is it a 10 or is it a 1?

The problem with the "problem" holds true for every sector. For example, a talented needlepoint artisan once shared with Lou her plans to launch a start-up selling high-end, custom-made needlepoint products. The item she expected to emerge as a bestseller was a needlepoint cellphone case with a thin pocket designed to hold a credit card. She generously gifted one to a mutual acquaintance, and while the acquaintance loved its look and craftsmanship, she thought the casing was too thick for the many people who like to keep their phones in their back pocket. Lou passed this feedback on to the entrepreneur who replied, "Well, she'll just need to get over that."

Instead of using feedback from a potential prospect in her target market and approaching the creation of her product from the customer's perspective, the needlepoint artisan was expecting the customer to adapt to what she had already created.

This reaction from founders is far more common than you might think. Sometimes it takes a phone being thrown at your head to clearly understand your users' pain point.

Jason Lieblich, Reflectent Software: Understanding the End User's Perspective

The traders swarming around technical support specialist Jason Lieblich on Wall Street's Credit Suisse First Boston trading floor were under pressure to quickly and accurately execute millions of dollars in transactions. The year was 2000, and banks like Credit Suisse relied on custom-developed software to facilitate their trades. Jason was tasked with keeping technical issues at bay. Peering up from their desks at a bank of computer screens, the traders diligently calculated potential gains and losses before selecting and entering their trades. But there were problems with the custom application, which sometimes failed to confirm their transactions were moving through the system. In such instances, the risk of assuming a trade was in process was too big, and they would need to cancel and resubmit it, during which time millions of dollars could be lost.

As Jason and other IT support staff jumped in to correct the process, it wasn't uncommon for particularly frustrated traders to pelt them with whatever was at hand—pens, staplers, note-books, or the telephone receivers anchored to their desks by a 15-foot-long cord. Jason was experiencing the traders' pain point. The application designers, he reasoned, were removed from the trading floor and didn't fully understand how their product worked in a hyperenergetic environment. Jason, however, understood both how the application had been written and what was playing out in real time and vowed he could do better.

Jason's start-up, Reflectent Software, was born out of these insights. Launched in 2002, its software application EdgeSight alerted IT support to problems before the users experienced them. In 2006, Citrix Systems acquired Reflectent Software for $24 million.

But for the success of every Reflectent, there are way more WayScripts.

WayScript: So Much Potential

A few years ago, Lou worked with a first-time entrepreneur who led the launch of WayScript, a promising start-up focused on the highly lucrative software development tools market. With its exponential growth in the global marketplace, investors were actively searching within this space for the next big thing.

WayScript chose to pursue a product-led growth (PLG) strategy by offering users initial access to their toolset for free. They reasoned that users would become dependent on the toolset's many features and pay a premium subscription after the six-month trial period ended. So, when thousands of developers began to download and extensively use the free toolset, venture capitalists took notice. WayScript raised millions in funding.

In anticipation of their success, the founders invested in lots of swag. Their logo—a purple mask resembling one a superhero might wear—was emblazoned on T-shirts, water bottles, and towels. Unfortunately, the founders and investors realized too late that WayScript had failed to adequately confirm whether users would be willing to pay to upgrade after the free trial ended.

Existing products on the market were equally adept at offering a solution, and WayScript simply didn't offer enough unique value to compete against more established contenders like Microsoft's GitHub, which is now the industry standard. WayScript then tried the traditional top-down sales approach of selling directly to large corporations, but they failed to build sales momentum, which ultimately led to their demise.

WayScript's failure offers an important lesson. It's easy to mistake general interest in a product with the public's willingness to actually purchase it from a nascent start-up. If you don't do the hard work up front to determine the weight of the problem and how much your target audience is willing to pay to solve it, investors' money will eventually run out, and you won't be able to raise any more capital.

In the end all you may have left is a lot of swag.

1.2 Bill Warner: Revolutionizing Video and Film Editing

Bill Warner, a pioneer in the field of digital, nonlinear editing is the embodiment of the entrepreneur who solved a problem by living it. In the process, his invention revolutionized an entire global industry.

In 1989, Bill Warner's start-up Avid Technology Inc. (Nasdaq: AVID) debuted the Avid Media Composer, the world's first digital, nonlinear video editing system that captured the full 30 frames per second signal.[1] Up until that time, editing consisted of physically cutting and splicing together pieces of film or copying segments of video and creating a new master tape. When using video, the editing process could be done only in a linear sequence. Simply put, editing was tedious and time-consuming with limited options.

Thanks to Bill's invention, the *Titanic* and *The Matrix* movies, two of the early cinematic productions to use Bill's digital editing system, dazzled audiences worldwide.[2] By 2000, approximately 100 movies and television programs were using the Avid Media Composer, securing its role as the industry standard. Eighteen years later, usage expanded to include 70% of commercially published music, 90% of original content from top streaming providers, and 9 out of 10 leading international news networks. In recognition of these feats, Avid was awarded two Oscars, one Grammy, and sixteen Emmys. Bill was inducted into the National Inventors Hall of Fame in 2019.[3]

Bill's entrepreneurial journey could have taken him on a very different path when, in 1973, he chose to major in economics at Washington University. His head told him it was the logical field to pursue, and his parents were pleased with his decision.

But fate intervened. It would take Bill breaking his back to follow his heart.

A Life-Changing Accident   Bill's life changed forever in February 1974 when the car he was driving hit a patch of ice and slammed into a tree.

While being treated at New York Medical Center, Bill roomed with Tom, a quadriplegic who was completely paralyzed in all four limbs. Yet Tom, who was close in age to Bill, refused to feel sorry for himself. Despite the physical trauma, his luminous personality remained intact. "Rooming with Tom was a real eye-opener," said Bill. "Even with a broken back, I became acutely aware that I had so much to be thankful for. Tom put everything in perspective for me."

Bill witnessed Tom's frustration at being unable to turn the lamp by his bedside on and off and knew he could help. So, he purchased a commercial product called the "Whistle Switch" that worked by squeezing air from a bulb. Bill removed the bulb and hung a plastic whistle for Tom to use. When he hooked the invention to the lamp, Tom blew into the whistle, and it went on. "His smile lit up the room," recalls Bill.

This experience led Bill to invent the Whistle System, which translates a regular audible whistle into one of eight commands that include turning a light, TV, telephone, stereo, and fan on and off. The Whistle System was recently displayed at the National Inventors Hall of Fame Museum.[4]

From the time Bill was young, he'd been interested in technology. As a child he was hooked on *Star Trek* and waited in anticipation for new Friday night episodes As an adult revisiting the series he appreciated its philosophical focus on humanism serving as a guiding principle.

"Spock embraced logic, but Kirk always followed his heart," says Bill. "It was time for me to do the same. Before the accident I'd made decisions based on who I thought I was supposed to be. The positive side effect of the accident was that it liberated me from this mindset. I gave myself permission to cut out all the crap. I wanted to be an engineer and an inventor. I wanted to be me."

The Problem Rears Its Head   Bill made good on his promise to himself. In 1980, he graduated from MIT with a Bachelor of Science in Electrical Engineering (BSEE). He eventually joined Apollo Computer to market 3D graphic workstations. A few years into his marketing role a beloved hobby would morph into a new work assignment and lay the groundwork for the founding of Avid Technology.

The idea for the Avid Media Composer grew out of Bill's love of photography. There was something about photography's ability to tell and preserve stories that resonated within him. At age six he was gifted a Kodak Brownie camera and graduated to a Nikon FTN in his teens. A video camera became his faithful companion once a model hit the market that was small enough for him to carry around. In his early thirties, Bill scripted a production called *Take the Money and Run* and, at a family gathering, relatives of all ages took part in it.

Now, in his parent's home, the problem that would change the course of Bill's life reared its head. He was discovering firsthand how cumbersome and time-consuming the editing process could be. Bill had connected his video camera to the family tape deck and copied segments of one tape to the other. Once copied, it was virtually impossible to make any further edits. A digitized editing solution had to be out there, he reasoned, if you had enough money to buy it.

Isn't This Supposed to Be Digital?   Recognizing the limitations of paper brochures as a marketing tool, Bill pitched his boss at Apollo Computer the idea of his heading up a video shoot showing the 3D graphic workstation in action. Bill's request was met with enthusiasm. Bill finally had the funds to hire the biggest postproduction house in Boston with the most sophisticated equipment being used at that time. He arrived at their door with stacks of time-coded videos shot on 3/4th inch videotape in hand. He was eager to learn how a digital system worked and requested the staff teach him how to run it. They sat him down and told him P was for play, the spacebar was stop, and R was rewind. But when Bill hit R, a tape deck rewound an analog tape deck.

Bill asked, "Isn't this supposed to be digital?" "Yes, the control of the tape decks is digital," came the reply. Frustrated, Bill asked, "So what good is that?" He was told the control deck was frame accurate and could easily fix individual frames. But no, it couldn't edit changes at will. And no, they weren't aware of the existence of a digital, nonlinear editing system. For Bill, the experience was a huge disappointment.

Apollo's sales team was thrilled with Bill's video. With its positive impact on sales, Apollo now wanted both existing and new products to have their own promotional video. Bill embraced the opportunity, but his editing needs quickly grew more complex. His initial strategy was to wait a couple years for a solution to hit the market. But as he made more videos, his frustration grew. By May 1987, he could stand it no more. At the end of a particularly grueling linear editing session, Bill informed his editor he was done.

What Bill had in mind was an editing system that could cut and paste full-motion video just like a word processing program cuts and pastes text. This would give the editor the opportunity to make many changes quickly and completely avoid the linear video editing process. Now, he needed to create a prototype.

In 1999, the Academy of Motion Picture Arts and Sciences presented Avid Media Composer inventor Bill Warner with the Oscar® for his transformation the editing process in filmmaking.
Photo Credit: Courtesy of Bill Warner.

The Power of a Prototype In 1988, Bill and a team of engineers recruited from Apollo prepared to present two prototypes of Avid/1 Media Composer,[5] an early version of Media Composer, at the National Association of Broadcasters annual conference. Bill rented a suite and invited video editors from across the industry to attend. He also extended an invitation to Bill Kaiser, an up-and-coming venture capitalist whom he'd worked with at Apollo. Both prototypes resonated with video editors, and requests came in for purchases once the product was created. Kaiser, too, saw its potential and committed $500,000. Avid had secured its first round of funding.

In 1987, Avid Technology set up shop in Burlington, Massachusetts, with Bill assuming the role of president and chief executive officer (CEO). Avid first found success in the television commercials market while developing and improving their software and hardware products. Avid's solutions are still used worldwide in today's film, television, music, and broadcast industry.

In March 1999, Bill took to the stage at the 71st Academy Awards ceremony to accept an Oscar for the concept, system design, and engineering of Avid Technology's Film Composer® and its lasting impact on the film industry.[6]

"Perhaps the most satisfying result is knowing that every single day something you've invented is being used and impacting people's lives," says Bill.

Beyond Avid Bill had stepped down as Avid's CEO in 1991 and remained connected to his start-up as a member of their board of directors until 2005. In 2023, Avid Technology was acquired by an affiliate of Symphony Technology Group (STG) for $1.4 billion.[7]

But his entrepreneurial journey was only starting. Bill went on to found multiple start-ups including Wildfire Communications and created Co-Flow Investing, LLC, an entity for direct investing in early-stage start-ups.

A passionate mentor, Bill often says to up-and-coming entrepreneurs, "They say necessity is the mother of invention. Well then, who's the father? I say that frustration is the father of invention because it's from frustration that necessity is born."

1.3 How to Attain Secondhand Knowledge of the Problem

So, what if you do have a really good idea for a start-up or a new product line within a mature company but you haven't directly lived the problem like Bill and Jason did? This doesn't mean you should forgo launching your venture. You do need, however, to delve into extensive and objective market research and speak with as many potential prospects and customers you can find. This is crucial in confirming an actual need for your product or service and whether it can attract a large market.

But how do you conduct research without potentially giving away your idea? This is a risk you have to take. While it is important to file for intellectual property protection for your idea, it is rare that the winner in the market always gets awarded a patent. Far more important is winning in the market. What counts most is securing customers faster than your competitors.

We recommend talking to at least 100 people and asking them all roughly the same questions. If you are launching a business-to-consumer product, you need to talk to 200 to 300 more. You need *a lot* of data and insights to understand if the problem you aim to solve is actually worth solving.

It's crucial to avoid asking "Mom Test" questions. The term was coined by Rob Fitzpatrick who wrote a bestselling book with the same name.[8] Just because your mom, who is perhaps your biggest fan, thinks your idea is good doesn't mean it will succeed.

Your goal is to determine what level of "pain" your potential customers are experiencing because they don't yet have your prospective product or service.

Is there enthusiasm in response to your idea? If the people you are speaking with had to rank their problems, would the one you aim to solve make it into the top one or two on a scale of ten? If there isn't enough real pain present, your target market has most likely found another product or service good enough to solve the problem. You may even discover that the people you speak with aren't experiencing the problem you're setting out to solve.

After interviewing friends and family members, lean into your professional social networks and organizations you belong to. Ask your connections if they'll take 15 minutes to discuss your business idea. After you've exhausted these connections, you must do the hard work of cold-calling or sending cold outbound email messages to your potential prospects. You may think your idea is great, even revolutionary, an obvious winner. But your prospects are busy people, and getting access to their time is difficult. If you do connect, it's important you ask these professionals the same series of questions. On a scale of 1 to 10, how would you rate this idea? Every company or organization has a budget for the current fiscal year, so you are asking for unbudgeted money to make your first sale—is your idea worthy of their doing so? Or is it good enough to divert *budgeted* money to fund buying your product? This last question is key to discovering the value of your idea.

Unfortunately, many founders don't want to take on this difficult work—or they elect to outsource it to someone else. This is a big mistake. Founders may not want to experience a lack of enthusiasm among their test audience or find out that their product doesn't solve real, pressing problems. But this discovery stage is crucial before you sink time and money into a venture without a big enough problem to solve.

Building Your Go-to-Market Sales Playbook

In the many years that Lou has taught at top universities, he's observed a distinct pattern among students interested in launching start-ups. They typically begin by incorporating their start-up followed by building a product, raising capital, and then figuring out how to sell it. But a few years after graduation, many founders are unable to sell their products or services at the level they need for their start-up to survive. Unable to raise more capital, their company ultimately closes. This sequence of incorporating, building a product, raising venture capital, and then learning how to sell is illogical. Why not figure out if the product is saleable *before* starting a company?

In 2020, Lou launched an HBS course called Entrepreneurial Sales so students could learn if their product was saleable before graduation. In it, students make cold calls, send cold emails, and participate in other activities to secure meetings with prospective customers. They then share the results of their prospecting work with the class.

Students record their prospective sales calls—always with permission granted beforehand—and play them back to the class, a process referred to as a *film review* session. A classmate is assigned to identify the strengths of the call, and another is asked where improvements could be made. But first, the students who make the calls self-assess. Those who receive responses to their cold emails ask the class how they should respond to transition the prospect into a customer.

Film reviews serve several purposes. First, the practice sessions demystify the process of selling. Second, students get feedback

from peers, which often helps them improve their calling techniques. In the process, they can better determine if the problem
they aim to solve will appeal to a large enough customer base to
justify the creation of a start-up. Some students discover their
ideas won't fly. It's better for them to learn this before graduation
rather than spending a lot of time and money post-graduation on
a fruitless venture. Others learn that their idea is indeed good
enough. In fact, many students have closed their first customer
contracts during the course.

The purpose of creating your own playbook is twofold: to
verify that your idea is worthy of your time, money, and energy
and, if so, to develop a step-by-step instruction guide for your
future sales team to follow. Here are the key elements you will
need to build out:

1. **A summary of the best way to take your product or service to market:** Ask yourself: should you sell your product or
   service directly to customers or through channel partners?
   The advantage of using a channel partner is their ability to
   tap into larger markets through their existing relationships.
   Or should you attempt to sell it through an original equipment manufacturer (OEM) who would sell your product
   through their brand name? These are just a few of the ways
   to take your product to market.

2. **A summary of the steps in your sales process:** The four key
   areas you need to identify are:

   (1) How will customers become aware of your product?

   (2) How will you demonstrate your product to potential
       customers?

   (3) How will customers sample your product or use it on a
       trial basis?

   (4) How will they purchase it?

You can now build on your sales process around these four steps, which will bring predictability into the process. However, if you do not develop a sales process, expect your sales to happen only randomly.

3. **Sample email templates:** Include the most successful cold email correspondences from your discovery process to serve as templates to generate future inbound sales leads.

4. **A product presentation:** Create a presentation to clearly explain what your product or service does and its fundamental value proposition.

5. **An analysis of competitive products or services on the market:** Conduct research to find out how people are solving problems with the products/services currently on the market. There's a temptation to believe you have no competitors—this is highly unusual. Competition actually proves that there's a market for what you're trying to sell. Your goal is to prove your offering's unique value from competitive solutions.

6. **Questions for sales hires to ask prospects:** Questions should address whether your product is a "must have" solution or a "nice to have" solution. The former indicates whether a potential customer needs to solve the problem now. It's also important to determine if a lead in a corporate setting has the authority to bring in a new, as yet unproven product. If they don't have the authority to decide on the allocation of funds for the purchase of your product or service, you can keep their name on file for future marketing purposes, but they aren't a qualified lead for a dedicated sales effort.

Avid Technology: Go-to-Market Playbook Case Study

In the early days of Avid Technology, the company launched by Bill Warner, the Avid Media Composer seemed ideal for editing in multiple categories: motion pictures, television short-form and long programs, documentaries, broadcast news, corporate videos, and standard 30-second television commercials. But while their breakthrough digital nonlinear editing system intrigued editors across the board, Avid was aware of their early limitations. In 1990, their digital editing system cost 25–30 percent more than purchasing an analog editing system. And while Avid used software compression, a process that reduced the size of files to save storage space and quickened data transfer, this trade-off on size and speed resulted in grainy, highly pixelated images.

Avid thus chose to pursue production companies creating 30-second television commercials to establish a beachhead market while continuing to improve upon their technology. If they had used the GTM playbook approach, the recommendation would have been to initiate 100 conversations with 100 production companies and ask them all the same set of questions. To start, Avid would have needed to lean into its network to make introductions including contacts made at tradeshows along with making cold calls to those outside their network. Questions would have sounded like this:

1. "When I speak to people who edit TV commercials, they tell me they'd like to have a way to make more versions of commercials to offer customers more options, but I don't suppose this is a problem for you?"

2. If they answer yes, the next question would be something like, "Okay, what is the business implication of not being able to offer your customers more versions of the same commercial?" Remember not to pitch your product when a customer shows interest, as tempting as this is. Try to understand the business implications of not solving this problem first.

3. If the answer is no, they're likely not a good prospect. This can help you understand that your product concept may not be suitable or a good fit for this particular set of customers.

4. Assuming the prospect says yes, the next question might be something like, "On a scale of 1 to 10, how important is it to you to solve this problem as soon as possible?"

5. If the customer says it's a 10 out of a 10, it is time for you to describe your product to them and ask if they would like to see a demonstration.

6. If the customer says it's a 1 out of 10, tell them rather than waste their time, you will stay in touch and offer to help them if you can. If they are not a prospect for your product, it's best not to spend a lot of time with them.

By leaning into their network and making cold calls, Avid did indeed confirm that the needs of 30-second television commercial editors were the most compatible. First, they discovered that commercial editors could adjust their workflow into a two-step process that created a finished, high-quality version of the commercial. Second, 30-second commercials also meant storage needs were minimal, which reduced hefty storage costs. Most importantly, editors could now make 10 times the number of ads for their clients to choose from in the same amount of time that analog editing took to create one version. The end result was greater customer satisfaction.

Tom Ohanian, an early Avid employee and author of *Digital Nonlinear Editing*[9] recalls, "Feature films and television shows shot hours and hours of footage and would fill up the drives in no time. Television commercials, by contrast, had on average 40 to 50 minutes of footage, which could be loaded into the system affordably. The advantages of using digital, nonlinear editing outweighed these limitations, giving the television commercial industry too many advantages to ignore."

The global market for 30-second television commercials was large enough to help Avid grow their sales to $100 million before focusing on the other use cases for the product. Within Avid's first 10 years their technology improved to the point where all the customer types they initially considered were adapting their editing processes to use the Avid Media Composer. But had Avid, with their initial technological limitations, tried to sell to everyone who had expressed interest, they most likely would have failed.

Entrepreneurs instinctively want to sell to everyone interested in their product to prove it has a large, addressable market. However, discovering which initial set of customers to target will take time and energy. Bill Aulet, managing director of the MIT Martin Trust Center for Entrepreneurship and author of the bestselling book *Disciplined Entrepreneurship: 24 Steps to a Successful Startup*, notes that having a disciplined approach to sales is key to establishing a beachhead market. He wisely sums it up: "The single necessary and sufficient condition for a business is a paying customer."

The Problem with the "Problem" in Mature Companies

Once a company achieves scale with its original product, growth eventually slows down. As a result, companies must constantly revise and alter their products to meet the demands of multiple market segments. The cost of servicing a large installed customer base means a company cannot rapidly iterate on new products. This notion of prioritizing "obligation over opportunity" is relevant in large companies.

It's tempting for product managers who are tasked to find ways to extend product growth to add on to an existing product that's done well. What better way to retain an existing customer base while attracting new users? It depends on the approach and the product.

Microsoft successfully followed this playbook with the debut of their Office suite in 1988. Their spreadsheets, presentation, and word processing tools, in all their iterations, are still the suite's core products. This strategy, if successful, has the added benefit of preventing competing companies with single-point solutions from making inroads into the market. For example, if a company comes up with a better version of PowerPoint, Microsoft can fall back on their "bundling" strategy and offer any of these point products for free. This is similar to what WayScript discovered too late in the sales process. So did a maturing Avid Technology.

Doubling Down on a Winner

While most companies dream of going public, it brings with it new pressures to extend their product lines. This happened to Avid Technology in 1994. While Avid's core editing product ran on the Apple McIntosh, management was aware that the market for Windows users was much larger. As a result, there was a push to port the Avid Media Composer to Windows and even more powerful hardware platforms.

At the time, Silicon Graphics (SGI) was the leading workstation vendor. Without in-depth knowledge of the end user's pain point or research to accurately determine market size, Avid announced a version of the Avid Media Composer called Spectrum that was compatible with SGI.

Some of Avid's sales team jumped into action and closed deals even before the Media Composer had been ported to the SGI hardware. But outside of a few high-end customers, they discovered there wasn't much demand for the product. Thus, Spectrum was discontinued before it had even shipped. Avid had run headlong into the problem with "the problem."

Here's what mature companies should do: analyze whether a new product will attract enough of a customer base to justify the creation of its own start-up, because if your proposed offering is viable only as a stand-alone product in a larger, multiproduct company, you increase your risk of the product failing to stand on its own.

Shaking It Up: The Job to Be Done Theory

In Clayton Christenson's book *Competing Against Luck*,[10] he introduces the "job to be done theory."[11] Rather than focusing on what customers are currently purchasing or their stated preferences, Christenson stresses that entrepreneurs need to understand the underlying priorities motivating consumers' behaviors and choices and the core essence of what drives sales.

In his book, Christenson cites the example of a fast-food company that hired him as a consultant to understand why their milkshake sales were flat. Did they lack enough flavors or perhaps they weren't being correctly priced? Christenson's firm opted to go directly to the source and interviewed customers standing in line. What they learned was eye-opening.

Milkshake sales conjure up images of parents purchasing them for their children or young adults drinking them while socializing with friends. But it turned out that the fastest-growing segment at the franchise were commuters buying milkshakes for breakfast. Commuters were then asked about alternative food products they might consider purchasing. It turned out those with long morning commutes were seeking a breakfast source they could consume over the duration of their drive. Other food products would have been consumed too quickly. The longer lasting milkshake added pleasure throughout their tedious commute.

Christenson's methods revealed a target market the company hadn't even known existed. Now, they were positioned to market to this newly identified demographic.

Understanding Your Target Market's Reality

Be aware of the reflex to project your reality onto your target audience or assign traits to consumers that simply don't hold up under scrutiny. If you don't understand what it's like to walk in your target audience's shoes, you risk alienating them.

The remedy? Be constantly observing. Regularly engage in conversations with people unlike yourself and really listen to what they have to say. Be constantly reading and researching. Embrace your mistakes—they're your teachers, so learn from them. And most importantly, always keep an open mind. You don't know what you don't know until you do.

2

Delegate Sales at Your Own Peril

Why Founders Must Become the Chief Salesperson

2.1 Overcoming Your Disdain of Sales

Let's face it, sales has a horrible reputation. It's the only business function where people post "No Soliciting" signs that instruct you not to do it. Who's ever seen a "No Marketing," "No Finance," or "No Strategy" sign? Some organizations cannot even bring themselves to use the word, and titles for sales jobs are often obfuscated to mask their true role. In software companies sales representatives are called "business development representatives," while the financial industry has "financial services representatives." Nonprofits have adopted their own sales euphemisms as well including "donor cultivation," "membership engagement," and "support acquisition."

For a long time, this attitude toward sales was reflected in U.S. business school curriculums. While former HBS faculty member Doug Chung taught such topics as sales management and strategy, the business school didn't offer a dedicated sales course until Lou introduced his Tech Sales course in 2015, which was based on the tech sales course he taught at MIT Sloan from 2011 to 2021.

According to Frank V. Cespedes, a senior lecturer in the entrepreneurial unit at HBS and author of five books on sales and marketing, this pushback is due in part to colleges viewing sales as "trade-school stuff" versus a teachable college discipline. In the 2016 article "More Universities Need to Teach Sales" published in *Harvard Business Review*,[1] Frank and his co-author found that out of more than 4,000 U.S. colleges, fewer than 100 had sales programs or even sales courses. He tells us the needle hasn't moved very much since that time.

Today, sales is a skill that is essential for all founders to develop. Simply put, you cannot delegate sales. If you cannot master selling your start-up's product or service, there's no way you will be able to hire and manage an effective sales team, much less grow and expand the company, sell it, or take it public. But to master the art of selling, you first need to tackle your own disdain for and misconceptions about selling.

2.2 Welcome to Harvard Business School's Entrepreneurial Sales Course

Lou has been tackling sales-related misconceptions head on throughout his combined 20 years of teaching sales courses at HBS and at MIT Sloan. When he launched his first HBS sales course in 2015, forty students were enrolled. Currently, HBS offers four dedicated sales courses with an enrollment of more than 500 business school students.

Each semester Lou kicks off his Entrepreneurial Sales course with a viewing of the commercial featuring "ShamWow guy" Vince Offer pitching his amazing absorbent towels. Vince's smooth-talking, high-energy persona propelled sales of the ShamWow towels into the millions[2] after the infomercial's debut in 2007 with viewers and critics alike acknowledging his mastery of the pitch. As one viewer recently posted under a YouTube video of the original infomercial,[3] "Dude could be advertising death itself and I'd buy it from him."

Students have shared that while Vince's presentation is both entertaining and convincing, they experienced some discomfort being so blatantly pitched to. They wouldn't be nearly as convincing if they were in Vince's shoes, they say, and that sales should be left to smooth-talking performers—those born with a "sales gene."

Lou then shows a clip from the 1992 movie *Glengarry Glen Ross*[4] featuring Alec Baldwin as Blake, the brutal motivational speaker who degrades a real estate sales team for their low numbers while showing off the material success he's acquired by embracing the ABCs—Always Be Closing. The students' responses tend to be more emotional—they've glimpsed this type of salesperson before, the bully hiding behind flowery words who, when the mask slips, reveals a ruthless streak. They typically agree that if becoming like Blake is what it takes to morph into a successful sales manager, then, "Whoa, that's not for me!"

Lou assures students he won't ask them to emulate Blake or the ShamWow guy. But to get over their discomfort with the idea of selling, they'll need to experience—and perhaps initially fail at—pitching to a customer firsthand.

Divers Delight: A Fictitious Case Study

Lou assigns "Divers Delight," a fictitious case study written by Howard Anderson, founder of the Yankee Group and a former senior lecturer at MIT Sloan and HBS who currently teaches entrepreneurship at Brown University.

The students will play the role of the founder of Divers Delight, a start-up that's just come to market with its first product, a wetsuit made of individual nanotube filaments that keeps divers warmer by 45°F. While the technology was jointly developed for use by the U.S. Navy Seals, Divers Delight owns the worldwide patent rights. You hold a significant advantage over the competition, but having no direct competition comes at a price: you'll need to charge $400 per wetsuit versus the industry standard of $250. New technology typically sells at a higher price point, making it challenging to compete against commoditized, low-priced products sold through big-box retailers and online giants.

Lou will assume the role of Jake Stow, head of East Coast Divers' buying group, a scuba shop chain with 25 stores across New England. To stay competitive, East Coast Divers is feeling pressured to lower its prices. Jake doesn't suffer fools gladly. He's been burned previously by start-up companies that couldn't deliver or even stay in business. The students' goal is to persuade Jake to purchase 12 wetsuits for each store.

Don't "Show Up and Throw Up"

In the next class, Lou transforms into Jake Stow and greets students wearing a Red Sox hat and a cynical expression. Behind him, stuck to a large whiteboard, is a diving map of Cape Ann, a rocky peninsula on Massachusetts' North Shore that juts out into the Atlantic Ocean. He cold-calls students to take part in the pitching exercise, and they take turns joining him at the front of the class.

What happens next is the same thing that's happened every time for the past 11 years that Lou has engaged students in the roleplaying session. The students diligently memorize details about the wetsuit—the individual nanotube filaments, its ability to keep divers warmer by 45°F, the U.S. Navy Seal's role in its creation, the wetsuit's competitive edge in the marketplace—and repeat them back to him. Then they ask how many suits he wants to order. Memorably, one student seller didn't think to sit down in the chair next to Lou's and loomed over him while rattling off the wetsuit's features without giving him a chance to ask a single question. She ended the pitch with, "It's been great talking with you. How many suits will you order?"

In general, students talked for about 80% of the time and Lou's dive shop owner talked around 20%. No student in the many years Lou has taught the class has ever commented on the Red Sox cap or the colorful diving map. Not once.

In response, Lou and his co-instructor Mark Roberge, author of *The Sales Acceleration Formula*,[5] model a more effective way to sell. Mark starts by building rapport. Eyeing the baseball cap, he comments on the Red Sox's season, which engages Jake. He notices the dive map and asks Jake where he likes to dive. Then Mark asks about the state of the dive business, which gets him talking even more. In fact, Jake becomes downright animated.

In the process, Mark is learning about a potential customer's needs. In this version of role playing, Mark asks questions and talks 20% of the time while Jake speaks the other 80%. By learning and listening, Mark is in a position to propose a next step.

Instead of the typical "show up and throw up," they are discovering together if the product is the right fit. It feels like a conversation versus a sales pitch. Mark is building rapport and, in the process, illustrating that sales is a skill that can be taught. Sure, some people come by sales pitching naturally, but learning to sell doesn't have anything to do with inheriting a "sales gene"—it's a skill you can learn and improve upon by mastering best practices.

Founder as Chief Salesperson

To know how to sell a start-up's product or service, it's up to the founder to make the first 15 sales. Anything less is risky. Why 15? It typically takes this long to truly understand how to sell your product or service.

There's an expression called a *bluebird*, which is slang for a lucky sale, one that comes in faster than anticipated and is typically impossible to replicate. Just like a bluebird unexpectedly perching itself on your shoulder, it isn't going to stay there very long and will most likely never land on your shoulder again. Your first one, two, or three sales may turn out to be one-off interactions with early adopters. While encouraging, they don't necessarily lead to a repeatable sales process. By your fifteenth sale you've typically journeyed through all the stages of your sales cycle and now have a good idea of what it takes to sell to different types of customers. You've also accumulated enough data points to see all the permutations that customers go through on their buying journey.

Next, we'll meet the very definition of an unlikely entrepreneur whose embrace of sales helped propel him to the heights of entrepreneurial success.

Matthew Riley, who rose from typewriter repairman to one of the United Kingdom's most successful entrepreneurs.

Photo credit: Wayne Myers.

2.3 Matthew Riley, U.K. Telecoms Market Disruptor

In 1991, 16-year-old Matthew Riley, a typewriter repairman, was a familiar face at multiple firms' typing pools in the northern English city of Nelson. Typists were paid by word count, so when a typewriter broke down, it meant a reduction in their day's wages. Matthew would arrive promptly with a cheeky grin and a bag of tools in hand, and soon enough the silence of a broken typewriter was replaced by the clacking sound of keys.

Compulsory schooling in the United Kingdom ended for students at age 16 after which they would choose to take their Advanced Level exams—the standard qualification for attending college—or earn a General National Vocational Qualification certificate through an apprenticeship. Matthew opted for the latter. He'd long struggled with reading, writing, and spelling, along with other aspects of traditional classroom curriculum and welcomed hands-on learning. Later in life he would be diagnosed with dyslexia.

His father, a paramedic who drove an ambulance, and his mother, who worked at a call center, supported his decision. They had instilled in their son that success in life was earned. It would be up to Matthew to make his own way post-apprenticeship.

Matthew would wildly exceed everyone's expectations with the launch of Daisy Group—a company he founded out of his garage in 2001—that has since grown into the largest independent, business-to-business (B2B) unified communications company in the UK, providing businesses with broadband, Voice over Internet Protocol (VoIP), telephone systems, and IT solutions with 14 offices located across the country and a workforce of more than 4,000 people.

In August 2025, Virgin Media O2—with its 45.8 million broadband, mobile, TV and home phone subscribers, and 16,000 employees—announced its merger with Daisy Group.[6] Their new company O2 Daisy—which Matthew chairs—is valued at more than $3 billion.

So, what ignited Matthew's rise from typewriter repairman to a top United Kingdom entrepreneur? It all started with his embrace of sales.

The Art of the Sale   Matthew began his vocational training in 1990 at FH Brown, a supplier of office goods and equipment. Each day he would repair typewriters and fax machines. While he enjoyed his work, he was particularly intrigued by one group of employees—the sales team.

"The salespeople drove the nicest cars and wore expensive clothes and shoes," recalls Matthew. "They'd come back from winter vacations with suntans or stories about skiing down the trails of a distant mountaintop."

Meanwhile, Matthew was making around £27 per week and spending £5 of it on bus fares to and from his parents' home in Burnley, a city in northern England, to neighboring Nelson where the company was headquartered. His mother bought him his first workplace suit and tie to help him save money.

"When you don't have much money, you need to be aspirational. I was determined to join the sales team," says Matthew. "I asked my manager multiple times to give me a shot, and he finally relented."

Now, instead of fixing fax machines, Matthew was selling them.

"Chatting people up came naturally to me, and my success in sales came from a place of enjoying conversations with potential customers and learning more about them and their needs by asking open-ended questions," says Matthew. "While I was persuasive, I avoided a hard sell." His approach worked as evidenced by Matthew's growing sales numbers. To celebrate, he proudly purchased a pair of knight ranger sneakers and excessively polished them.

Scratching the Entrepreneurial Itch   From 1991 through 1997, the U.K. government transitioned the telecommunications market from a duopoloy—only British Telecom and Mercury Communications were licensed to carry telephony services over fixed links[7]—to open competition, recognizing that privatization would lower prices and offer people a wider choice of service providers.[8]

At FH Brown, Matthew began selling a new Panasonic telephone system to business offices. His sales numbers were so impressive that he was headhunted by Deutsche Telekom, which was gearing up to launch their own telephone system developed for call centers. Matthew's loyalties were with FH Brown—that is, until he was offered a salary triple of what he was currently earning in commissions. Soon enough, he won a top sales award for his performance at his new company. Not long afterward, he went skiing for the first time.

By the late 1990s, Matthew's confidence in his ability to sell opened him up to the idea of launching his own start-up. He reasoned that his sales know-how would be his guiding force in selling his own products, training salespeople, and assembling a top-notch sales team. By having climbed the ranks—at Deutsche Telekom he managed sales across the United Kingdom—he'd gained in-depth knowledge of tele- coms infrastructure and insights into international business practices. But while he understood the importance of the founder as chief salesperson, he knew he had more to learn about running a business before investing time, money, and energy into his own ventures.

"I became a sponge soaking up information on what makes successful companies tick," says Matthew. He asked colleagues up and down the ranks about their work, paid attention to how the company handled issues big and small, and explored why some companies were doing better than others. "All along the way I kept asking questions." Meanwhile, a burning desire to launch his own company grew.

Coming Up Daisies   Matthew embarked on his entrepreneur- ial journey by initially launching a few small businesses to, as he puts it, "cut my teeth." These included Daisy Executive Search & Selection in 1998 and Coms Care in 1999, which he sold in 2001.

With the dot-com bubble bursting and the recession that followed, it made sense that entrepreneurs might hesitate to launch a start-up. Not Matthew, who geared up for the launch of "the big one." While the risks were real, particularly with a mortgage and a young family to care for, Matthew says that he doesn't remember feeling nervous.

In 2001, Matthew launched Daisy Communications, a precursor to Daisy Group, from a desk in his garage. Six years later, after adding 22 more businesses to his portfolio, Matthew won two prestigious awards: the Ernst and Young's National Young Entrepreneur of the Year[9] and the Corporate Entrepreneur of the Year[10] awarded by the Bank of Scotland Corporate during the finale of their £25 million Entrepreneur Challenge.

Daisy Group went public on the Alternative Investment Market in the United Kingdom in July 2009. For many entrepreneurs, becoming a publicly traded company is the ultimate badge of honor. Some CEOs consider running a public company as a "varsity" business because of the strict regulatory requirements necessary to sell shares to the public. The transition from private to public company requires that the leaders surround themselves with a team that can achieve predictable results under the scrutiny of public inspection. In most cases, public financing offers the lowest cost of capital.

In November 2014, Matthew wisely recognized an opportunity to take advantage of better financing terms in the private capital markets and closed a deal that valued it at £494 million. As a private company, Matthew was able to grow Daisy with more flexibility and freedom than he could have had the company remained public.

In between going public and private, Matthew flirted with stardom in 2011 and 2012 when he appeared as a judge for two seasons on the United Kingdom's version of *The Apprentice*.[11]

His judgments came from a place of understanding both the marketplace and the intense pressure the budding entrepreneurs were under. Matthew was offered a third season, but he chose growing his business—his real passion—over show business.

Fast-forward to 2025 and Matthew is back making headlines with the news of his merger with Virgin Media O2, which, as Matthew shared with a U.K. *BusinessCloud* reporter, "blows any previous deals out of the water."[12] Just as Matthew was persistent in his attempts to join the FH Brown sales team, he says he pitched the idea of a merger with Virgin Media O2 five or six times over a ten-year period before it became official. His persistence was well worth it—combined, the company will have approximately 700,000 customers, annual revenues of around £1.4bn ($1.85bn), and a valuation of between £2.5bn ($3.30bn) and £3bn ($3.96bn), including debt,[13] and will be a challenger to the BT Group's longstanding dominance in the U.K. enterprise communications market.[14]

Paying It Forward Despite reaching impressive heights, Matthew remains true to his roots. With offices now located across the United Kingdom, Matthew has made a conscious decision to keep Daisy headquartered in Nelson, the city where he took the bus to his first job at FH Brown. In a region that had grappled with high unemployment rates, Daisy is now the area's top employer.

"I understand if a potential employee doesn't have any qualifications. So, we bring people from unskilled backgrounds to Daisy and train them. As a result, lots of families work here, and we appreciate their loyalty," says Matthew.

As a Fellow of the Prince's Trust, Matthew is committed to nurturing the next generation of business leaders, offering practical guidance and support to young adults embarking on their entrepreneurial journeys.

"I'm a great believer that if you can build it, you don't necessarily have to have immediate knowledge, because you can learn it and earn it."

Landing Your First Customer

We're not going to sugarcoat it—securing your first customer can be hard. You're up against other competitors who are equally determined to sell their products or services to your customer base. If you're attempting to sell to a business or vendor keep in mind that their budget has already been set at the beginning of the fiscal year, so you will, in essence, need to "steal" funding from an already allotted budget category.

If you've done your due diligence during the discovery stage as described in Chapter 1, "The Problem with the 'Problem,'" you've already identified your ideal customers, leveraged your network, and created a value proposition, among other important steps. You are better positioned for the task ahead. But the fact remains that the first buyer of your product or service is taking a risk in betting on your ability to deliver.

Two key determinants in convincing a first customer to bet on you are trust and expertise. Your odds of closing a deal improves when your first customer trusts you're looking after their needs with the objective of helping them to succeed through the implementation of your product or service. Your odds increase further if you are viewed as an expert in your field. Make sure to convey your expertise through multiple channels in a way that stresses your commitment to meeting customers' needs.

Two very successful women whose stories we are pleased to share next embraced different approaches to landing their first customers.

Elizabeth Elting, co-founder of TransPerfect.
Photo credit: Melanie Dunea.

2.4 Dream Big and Win: Landing TransPerfect's First Customer

Elizabeth "Liz" Elting is the co-founder of TransPerfect, which she launched in 1992 and grew into the world's largest provider of language services and related technologies.[15] Today it has more than $1.2 billion in annual revenue, operating in more than 140 cities around the globe.[16] Following her sale of the business 25 years after founding the company, Liz established the Elizabeth Elting Foundation, a nonprofit with a focus on advancing the economic, social, and political equality of women and marginalized people. With a net worth of approximately $450 million, Liz has secured a spot on Forbes' Richest Self-Made Women every single year since 2016.[17]

Liz's initial career path was far removed from the entrepreneurial journey. In 1987, she graduated from Trinity College with a B.A. in Modern Languages—Liz studied French, Spanish, Portuguese, and Latin—and planned to work for companies where her language skills would be an asset. But it was while she was employed at Euramerica Language Management, a large translation company based in New York City, that Liz realized she could improve upon their practices to deliver complex projects more quickly and accurately with a sharper focus on quality and client service. This realization was the catalyst for her enrollment in NYU's Stern School of Business MBA program where, in a dorm room, she and her co-founder fleshed out their plans for a service-minded end-to-end solutions translation enterprise, which they launched directly after her graduation.

To secure TransPerfect's first client, Liz hit the phones hard on day one. "The only way to generate sales was to pick up the phone and start calling," she remembers. "For many months I made 300 phone calls and sent out 300 pitch letters every single day."

Liz describes the moment she connected with her first client in her *Wall Street Journal* bestselling book *Dream Big and Win: Translating Passion into Purpose and Creating a Billion-Dollar Business*[18]:

> *"I'd just hung up from making my millionth cold call of the day when the strangest thing happened. The phone, which was hot to the touch from constant use, began to ring. For a moment, I was stunned that the phone could receive incoming calls, but I quickly pulled it together and answered the call."*
>
> *"The Demovsky Lawyer Service (DLS) was calling to see if we could accommodate a small job, translating a three-page contract into Slovak. I was torn between laughing and crying while speaking*

with DLS, but I somehow held it together, not only long enough to get all the job specifics, but also to find out how they'd heard about us. Turns out they'd received one of our mailings, and I'd had them tracked on our extensive spreadsheets. Instead of screaming, 'I can't believe we pulled this off!' I handled the call like it was one of a thousand I'd received that day. I didn't want them to know they were the guinea pig for all our processes. Instead, I acted like I'd been there before. And here's the thing—I sort of had. I'd been there for hundreds of Euro-America Translation clients, and what this client was asking for wasn't anything I hadn't managed previously. But this time, I owned it. I had a plan to work out the bugs. I had the benefit of handling the process from start to finish, to ensure a seamless, TransPerfect experience. It was only a couple of hundred dollars, but we were on our way."[19]

Liz's first sale highlights the importance of outbound prospecting. Her outbound sales efforts generated inbound sales leads, which typically close at a higher rate than outbound cold calls. So even though a prospect may not have a need for your product or service right now, they are "pre-aware" of you and may develop a need later. For Liz, most of her client base became repeat customers.

Liz implemented a cash-efficient model for growing sales. When she started out, she challenged herself with selling $50,000 in services per month for three consecutive months to hire and pay her start-up's first salesperson. When she met this goal, she decided to implement a "rule of $50K" and presented the new salesperson with the same challenge before they could hire TransPerfect's first sales assistant. Then, the two of them were tasked with selling $120,000 per month for three consecutive months in order to add a third person to their team and were then tasked with selling $190,000, and so on. As far as compensation, the initial salesperson would have a low draw but a high upside and earn 10% commission. This commission never sun-setted, so they would make the same 10% on the hundredth or thousandth project from a client as they did on their very first sale. Throughout her career, Liz remained relentlessly commit-ted to this winning formula.

While Liz's story reflects the importance of sheer persistence and outbound marketing in landing a first customer, the found-ing of Katie Couric Media (KCM) illustrates the importance of considering your first customer as a design partner to establish a strong foundation for future work. Here is legendary broadcast journalist Katie Couric and her husband John Molner's story.

2.5 How Katie Couric Media Landed Its First Customer

Katie Couric is an award-winning broadcast journalist whose career has spanned more than three decades. From 1991 to 2006, Katie co-anchored NBC's *The Today Show*, which was the top-rated morning program during her 15-year tenure.[20] Katie broke gender barriers when she became the first woman to solo anchor a network evening newscast, leading CBS Evening News from 2006 to 2011.While at CBS, she also served as a correspondent for *60 Minutes*. Katie has authored two *New York Times* best-selling books: *The Best Advice I Ever Got*[21] and her memoir, *Going There*.[22] In 2008, she and eight other women personally affected by cancer co-founded Stand Up to Cancer (SU2C), a nonprofit that has raised more than $800 million to support cancer research. With SU2C's support, the FDA approved nine new cancer thera-pies. This is among Katie's most proud accomplishments.

Katie is celebrated for her consistent ahead-of-the-curve reporting, her warm yet probing interview style, and her perse-verance and toughness in achieving multiple industry firsts.[23] She is a recipient of the duPont-Columbia University Award,[24]

Katie Couric and her husband John Molner.

Photo credit: Dorsey Studios.

Peabody Award,[25] two Edward R. Murrow Awards,[26] and a Walter Cronkite Award,[27] among others, and was twice named one of *Time* magazine's 100 most influential people.[28]

Now, with the 2017 launch of Katie Couric Media (KCM), which she co-founded with her husband John Molner, she's added entrepreneurship to her list of accomplishments. While Katie hadn't initially envisioned embarking on an entrepreneurial journey, she's embracing the independence and creative control that comes with owning a business.

Katie and John didn't make their decision to build a digital media company lightly. They recognized that they were launching their start-up against the backdrop of a crowded, fractured, highly competitive, and constantly morphing market space. While Katie's fame was an asset, it didn't guarantee success.

Name recognition is a double-edged sword. Yes, celebrities are better positioned to attract capital and capitalize on their name. On the flip side when celebrity ventures fail to gain traction, the resulting news coverage is often unduly critical and potentially damaging to their reputation. Regardless of money and fame, celebrities still need to understand all the intricacies and demands behind launching and scaling a start-up if they are to succeed. Otherwise, they risk becoming figureheads in a business run by outsiders whose intentions may differ from their own. And while a curious public may make initial purchases based on name recognition, building a repeatable business model means celebrities must create value for their target audiences.

Laying the Groundwork for Katie Couric Media   In 2016, Katie arrived at a career crossroads. For the past four years she'd served as Yahoo! News' Global News Anchor, a role that allowed her to pivot from legacy broadcasting into the rapidly growing realm of digital media. But as Yahoo! prioritized developing tech tools over investing in their journalism coverage, she realized it was time to move on.

Katie briefly considered returning to an established news network. But with broadcast and cable television under financial pressure, it wasn't clear if they'd be willing to invest in paying anchors to cover the type of stories and social issues that interested Katie. Of greater concern, network news audiences were declining, and more advertising dollars were shifting to digital media. With the advent of social media, cable, streaming, and other platforms, gone were the days of one network controlling a significant majority audience.

"Mass media is an oxymoron," says Katie.

An early adopter of social media, Katie had encouraged CBS executives to use social media platforms to engage a wider audience. But as one senior CBS executive told her, "It's beneath the anchor of the *CBS Evening News* to go on the Twitter."

Katie also craved creative control over the next stage of her career. Earlier that year she'd produced *Under the Gun*,[29] an acclaimed documentary examining gun violence and the failure of lawmakers to pass commonsense gun safety legislation, and, in 2014, *Fed Up*,[30] which explored the food industries' complicity in America's obesity epidemic. Despite numerous digital media competitors, she believed there was room for a digital media company producing such purposeful content, which could reach millions of people on growing social networks.

Katie's husband John Molner supported her idea from the start. Introduced in April 2012 by a mutual friend, the couple had immediately connected. With Katie's deep interest in cancer research, she'd initially asked their friend, who was married to a trauma surgeon, if she knew any single doctors. John, a mergers and acquisitions banker at a private investment firm, didn't fit this description. Says John, "When she learned I wasn't a doctor, Katie had joked, 'Does he have a pulse?'" Upon meeting, Katie loved John's dry and wry sense of humor, and their relationship blossomed.

John was an analytical investor with strong commercial instincts. After earning an MBA at the University of Chicago in 1990, he joined Brown Brothers Harriman (BBH), a New York–based, privately held investment firm. In 2001, he was named a general partner. Over the course of his 24-year career at BBH, he oversaw the firm's corporate advisory practice and advised clients across a range of industries in the United States, Latin America, and Europe. He also played a role in the firm's growing private equity investment business. Not that long after they met, John was contacted by a reporter who revealed their publication was going to run a story about their relationship. She'd asked John to comment, but he declined. "I was worried BBH wouldn't like the tabloid coverage, so I sat down with the firm's managing partner.

When I revealed the celebrity in question, he seemed relieved and said, 'Katie Couric . . . that's not a problem.'" About an hour after the news broke, BBH's website crashed due to excessive traffic from visitors searching for clues about their relationship.

John recognized that legacy broadcasting advertisement dollars were declining, while digital activity, in particular news consumption via cell phones, was on the rise. Monetizing digital audiences—measured in cost per thousands of website views—would be challenging for a start-up, even with Katie's name recognition.

John reflected on a screening he and Katie had attended in the fall of 2017 featuring Ken Burns' and Lynn Novick's new documentary series on the Vietnam War. After the lights dimmed, the screen displayed Bank of America's logo before the opening credits rolled.

"My first thought was, 'What does Bank of America have to do with Vietnam?'" recalls John "Then it became clear to me that Bank of America valued its association with elevated storytelling. Katie and I believed we could create a scalable business by developing brand partnerships with those interested in associating themselves with purposeful content. Together, we could build a large audience around causes that mattered to us and our brand partners."

While he and Katie believed there was an initial market to serve as their media business' primary building block, they envisioned a company—one they would name Katie Couric Media (KCM)—that would encompass a series of businesses built around storytelling that would support each other and be distributed across digital platforms.

They fleshed out an idea for a daily newsletter they would name *Wake Up Call* (*WUC*) to feature Katie's take on daily events. *WUC* would highlight a few daily top stories along with features focusing on health and wellness, lifestyle, and culture. They recognized that digital audiences might spend only a limited amount of time on a newsletter delivered via email, so the stories would need to be written with this form of news consumption in mind. An affiliate e-commerce business offering shopping recommendations—which developed into Katie's Shop with the tag line "Brands We Love"—and a platform for experiential/live events focusing on topics such as health and wellness that KCM would produce, would bring in "presenting sponsorships" in addition to charging attendees for admission.

"John and I were ready to build something together," says Katie. "I'm a storyteller, and John brings tremendous business acumen and a network of clients. And we truly trust each other, which is such a rare and special experience when working in the media. He was the type of trusted partner that I didn't have at other times in my career."

Intersecting Circles As John gave more thought on how to finance the new business, he thought of media executive Bill Koenigsberg, CEO of Horizon Media. When they met, John drew three intersecting circles on a piece of paper. He wrote "brand marketing" in the first circle, "storytelling" in the second, and "community" in the third. In the space where the three circles intersected, John wrote, "Katie Couric Media." John shared his belief that brands and storytelling were converging to stand for causes in addition to making an attractive return on investor capital. Then he asked Koenigsberg, "Wouldn't brands want to be associated with curated, purposeful content that could drive a community that valued Katie's ability to tell a story?"

Koenigsberg recognized how John and Katie's complementary skills would make this business model work and committed to funding their initial investment round. John then raised more capital from a small group of investors from three principal areas—media, tech, and private equity investors—who, he believed, would be able to provide insight and guidance as they navigated the challenges of starting a business in a highly competitive landscape. Within two years, all investors earned back their initial capital and retained their equity position.

Choosing the Right First Partnership   With funding and a management team in place, Katie was eager to start making impactful content under the KCM brand. But she and John instinctively knew they needed to select their first customer carefully to establish a strong foundation for future work. John developed a list of brands that spent considerable money on advertising and that were closely identified with important corporate social responsibility (CSR) initiatives. KCM wanted to avoid partnering with a brand that could only provide a one-off contract. KCM's audience demographics were also an important consideration.[31]

Years earlier, Katie had met Marc Pritchard, the award-winning chief brand officer of Proctor & Gamble, at a *Glamour* Woman of the Year award dinner where Katie was among the honorees.[32] Pritchard respected Katie's journalistic integrity and her ability to analyze and report on current issues relevant to consumers, and Katie viewed Marc as a person of integrity who routinely set the course for the marketing industry. "I thought that since KCM had an outstanding journalist at the helm we needed an equally exceptional partner. Marc and P&G fit the bill," says John. He and Katie arranged a meeting with Pritchard and shared their business plan and vision for KCM.

"We told Marc we wanted to create highly engaging content that people would care about," says John. "And we wanted a brand partner who felt the same way."

John says their value proposition included a set of "content deliverables" and media impressions across their platforms; helping P&G to connect to other important voices/experts/ influencers who fit into conversations they could potentially develop together; and the support of fast-changing "communication" priorities. John explains, "All of sudden 'a fire is burning somewhere'—how can KCM help shine a light on issues important to P&G and our national audience?"

John priced the contract in a way that recognized P&G was not only a customer but also a "design partner." KCM assigned an account manager to P&G to better understand how to connect KCM's content to P&G's corporate social responsibility (CSR) goals. For example, one well-known P&G brand, Oral B, made progress on what the company called the "smile gap" by donating oral healthcare products to underserved communities.[33] When their annual contract came up for renewal, John says P&G suggested they move their agreement to a multiyear deal.

"We're proud of our relationship with P&G, which continues to be one of our most important brand relationships," says John. "Likewise, we're proud of what we've accomplished with Marc Pritchard and his team at P&G."

Building Your Relationship with Early Customers

Many founders imagine they need to close their first customer at a maximum list price to prove the value of their product. But KCM offers a textbook example of how to instead partner with a first customer. Offering a discount to early customers in exchange for learning what's most important to them makes it more likely they'll become ardent users of your product as well as having them serve as a reference. In KCM's case, having P&G as a reference helped close subsequent contracts with big brand companies like Mars, Humana, Google, Pfizer, and Exact Sciences.

By landing their first customer, John developed an understanding of KCM's sales process, which was reinforced when he secured the next 10 customers. It was only after documenting the sales process that he hired sales professionals to augment his efforts.

Katie Couric Media Today   Fast-forward to 2025, and KCM is a growing, diversified digital media company delivering content each week through its multiple platforms to more than five million followers and subscribers of their six newsletters and YouTube channel. KCM has developed dozens of significant content partnerships with global brand partners, and their work staff has grown to nearly 50 employees. Katie's Shop, their e-commerce business under the KCM umbrella, has featured 100-plus affiliate companies. Katie's podcast *Next Question* has produced 170 episodes over seven seasons with nearly 30 million downloads and has been repositioned as a YouTube channel. KCM now sells a mix of media placement to clients in addition to their subscriber-based newsletters.

John says KCM's live stream events, which bring together thought leaders and experts, is an increasingly important part of their overall business in driving engagement. KCM also repurposes aspects of these events to create additional digital content to be distributed to larger audiences across platforms.

While the company doesn't disclose financial information, John tells us KCM has achieved profitability in every quarter since its launch, and annual revenue and operating profit per employee are higher than peer benchmarks. KCM's website, www.katiecouric.com, which aggregates content from KCM newsletters, podcasts and events, receives more than one million unique visits per month and three million page views.

"Before we launched KCM, I never saw myself as an entrepreneur. Yet, throughout my career, I've always taken risks that I'm proud of," says Katie. "I continue to enjoy building a team of talented and driven people who are really invested in our mission to help people understand our complex world, and working with our brand partners who align with us on purposeful content. And I love connecting with audiences on topics we mutually care about. Scaling a thoroughly modern media company gives me enormous freedom and flexibility. And it's gratifying to be 'the boss of me' . . . except, that is, when Molner tries to keep me in line!"

2.6 Building Your Sales Culture

Daisy, TransPerfect, and KCM all illustrate the importance of founders making their company's initial sales and becoming comfortable with selling. But more often than not, founders delegate sales to another person. They may be uncomfortable with the thought of selling. They may attempt a couple sales calls before giving up. Or they may think they're too busy with other start-up demands to take it on. But founders who chose to delegate sales do so at their own peril.

Crucially, learning how to sell helps you influence the *culture* of your company's sales organization. A sales culture is a series of values and collective attitudes your sales team develops and puts into action, which becomes an informal way your sales team works together and conducts business. Whether intentional or not, sales culture develops over time. By delegating sales to an outside leader, founders inadvertently invite the sales leader to establish their own sales process and sales culture, which could be at odds with what they envision.

Most concerning, some sales leaders given *carte blanche* in running the sales team create a corrosive culture, isolating customers from the rest of the company. By isolating other departments from customers, the sales team becomes the "owner" of customer relationships, placing them in a position of power.

When a sales team has undue influence over finance, it may lead to harm. For example, sales quotas are set between sales and finance, balancing new revenue with operating expense planning. While it's common to have higher commissions once a sales rep achieves their quota, the sales quotas may instead be set based on what a top sales rep may demand to be paid rather than as a function of sales capacity.

So, rather than delegating sales, we recommend co-creating a sales culture with your head of sales. And you can't do that unless you, too, know how to sell. By learning to manage the first salesperson directly, you'll better understand the basics of sales management, which is important to know before making such hires as a vice president of sales or chief revenue officer. Co-creating a sales culture also provides the opportunity for you and your sales leader to map a sales compensation plan together based on how your new customers move through their buyer's journey.

Often, a first step for a newly hired sales leader is to reuse the same sales compensation plan from their previous company. The "cut-and-paste" reflexive action may seem logical; why create new compensation plans for your company's sales team if the one at the previous company worked so well? But each company's sales process and go-to-market design are unique to them and their newly found customers. By working together you can better match your product to your customers.

In his *Harvard Business Review* article, "The Sales Learning Curve,"[34] co-author Mark Leslie, co-founder of Veritas Technology and a lecturer at Stanford Graduate School of Business, stresses that as your organization grows, all employees will benefit from learning how customers acquire and use your product. We agree—by creating enthusiasm among your staff and providing them with a common language to talk about your products and services, you will better position everyone in your organization to convey your value proposition.

2.7 Turning Around the Root Causes of Failure in Sales

During any given week, Lou is contacted by founders, board members, or investors asking for his help. The conversation typically opens with the person discussing the merits of a company and its great potential. When Lou asks why they think he could help, their voice drops almost to a whisper. "Well actually, the company has a sales problem." They say this as if the company is in a surprisingly unique situation. It isn't.

Every company Lou has ever worked with has experienced sales problems at some point. Sometimes business leaders think they're experiencing a forecasting problem. But problematic forecasting is only a symptom of a larger problem. Lou's diagnosed five root causes of sales problems:

1. Improper sales qualification
2. Failure to adopt a sales methodology
3. Failure to invest in sales enablement
4. Not having created a sales playbook
5. Lack of product-market fit

Any one of these problems can cause havoc. The following describes how to get it right from the outset.

Successful Sales Qualification: ABQs and BANT

Remember Blake from *Glengarry Glen Ross*? Rather than adopting Blake's ABC mantra, we recommend embracing the ABQs— Always Be Qualifying—but with one caveat: make it your goal to properly qualify a prospective customer. This is particularly crucial for start-ups who haven't yet hired professional salespeople. When someone is learning how to sell, it is easy to confuse a prospect who shows interest in a product with a prospect who's actually qualified to *buy* the product. Sure, you may have a great call with a potential customer, but what does that mean?

To create a foundational sales qualification system, we recommend using a rubric known as BANT,[35] which involves asking the prospect three questions:

Budget: Does the prospect's organization have the budget to make the purchase?

Authority: Is the prospect in a position of authority to make purchase decisions?

And what is their level of *need* and *timing*? Companies divide their annual budgets into quarters, so learning when purchases are made during the fiscal year is important.

If every sales rep asks the same questions, a founder can establish a common language for discussing prospects who'll eventually be part of a sales forecast. Too often, prospects who stay in your forecast but never close a deal risk becoming "forecast furniture." Like a sofa, these prospects just sit there, never moving on to become customers. Don't allow this to happen.

Adopting a Sales Methodology

To build consistency in your sales organization, all salespeople need to use a common system. There are many sales methodologies you may want to consider adopting, such as Sandler training,[36] the MEDDIC sales methodology,[37] SPIN selling,[38] and Challenger Sales methodology,[39] to name a few. Some sales methodologies are very good for transactional sales, while others are designed for enterprise sales. We recommend researching and choosing a methodology that best complements your company and then working with your sales organization to build a common language to describe how prospects will be converted into customers. Without a common language or way to refer to prospects, it is difficult to predict whether or when a prospect will buy your product.

Investing in Sales Enablement: Earning Your "Wings"

To build a repeatable sales process, founders must develop clear training and onboarding systems that explain to salespeople what their product or service does, why it's different from their competitors, and what skills they must master before calling on prospects. For example, at Black Duck Software, a company that helps clients manage security, quality, and license compliance risks, their head of enablement Chester Liu established "Flight School" where recent sales hires "earned their wings" while learning to sell the company's products. Black Duck then celebrated when a new class of salespeople completed training. This celebration became the first of many as graduates accomplished sales goals and progressed through the organization. But too many start-ups completely omit sales training as a foundational onboarding step or don't celebrate sales rep's accomplishments throughout each stage. No wonder they miss their forecasts!

Your Sales Playbook: Creating a Marching Band Versus a Virtuoso

As we shared in Chapter 1, creating a sales playbook is crucial to both your discovery process and creating an instruction guide for new salespeople to learn how to sell your company's products. Many start-ups assume a new salesperson will eventually figure out what works. This approach is flawed for several reasons. First, it lengthens the time it takes for a salesperson to "ramp" or become good enough to generate revenue to cover their own expenses. Second, even if a sales rep does "figure it out on their own," there's a risk that you've enabled a "virtuoso"—an individual sales leader who creates something brilliant and brings in money, but not necessarily something that's repeatable. By co-establishing a set of repeatable processes at the outset, your sales team becomes more like a marching band, playing in an organized way with each musician contributing to the music. Your goal is to create a sales team that moves to the same beat.

Achieving Product-Market Fit

Often a sales forecasting miss or poor sales execution isn't a sales problem at all; similar to a fever, it's a symptom of a larger problem. Product-market fit refers to the point where a start-up has moved beyond its earliest adopters to establishing itself in the marketplace with a repeatable sales process that supports growth and profitability. But founders may mistakenly believe they've tapped into a large enough market for their offering once they've raised a certain level of funding or have sold a sizable volume. A much better measure of product-market fit is when a considerable number of customers has successfully implemented your product and purchased more of it.

When you don't do the hard work early on in determining potential market size, you also risk hiring sales reps too soon whom you may eventually need to fire due to a lack of sales revenue. It's much more prudent to hire sales staff once you've established a clear return on investment.

Brewing Beer: A Metaphor for Scaling Your Start-Up

Nearly 5,000 years ago, the ancient Sumerians stumbled across an unusual phenomenon.[40] Water, barley, and hops left bubbling in the hot desert sun had fermented into a tasty concoction that created pleasant sensations in those who drank it. But this early beer often "skunked," leading to sickness and even death from spoilage. Over thousands of years, brewmasters developed tools and techniques to continuously improve the quality, taste, alcohol content, and color of beer. Yeast was introduced in the late 1800s. Refrigeration eventually led the way for the mass production and branding of beer. The Sumerians' accidental fermentation process has now morphed into a highly refined, predictable process, allowing modern brewmasters to predict the outcome of a batch in great detail.

Start-up founders must embark on the same journey, transitioning from a one-time sale to early sales to building a repeatable sales process and growing and managing a high-performing sales team.

While it's acceptable to spend a lot of money and time to acquire your first customer, investors in your business want to know how you will drive down your cost of sales over time and become more efficient in your sales process. This forces a series of questions unique to your company: should your company sell direct to customers or through retailers or wholesalers? If you choose the latter, you will need to address how to price your product for intermediaries, ensuring they make a profit selling your product. What type of salesperson should you hire—a direct seller or someone skilled at selling through partners? And how should you compensate your sales team?

This transition from happenstance to strategic growth and predictability takes time, diligence, and experimentation, a process founders are apt to misunderstand unless they've been directly involved in selling early on. By gaining deep insight into your sales process and cycle, you are better positioned to navigate whatever challenges life throws your way. *Cheers!*

3

Fundraising
It's Like Sales. Except It Isn't

3.1 You're Going to Need Cash

Fundraising is very much a sales job in that you're selling a compelling vision of your company's potential. Unlike sales, you are agreeing to return investors' money, ideally with a return on their investment.

Capital comes in many forms including loans from family, friends, and banks, as well as investments from angel investors and venture capitalists. In this chapter, we explore best practices in working with all of them. But first, we'll meet a small business owner who nearly passed on launching her business due to an initial lack of capital. But she persevered and went on to become an unlikely "tire queen."

3.2 Mary McLaughlin, Independent Tire

Sister Elinor Rose inadvertently set a teenage Mary McLaughlin (née Sullivan) onto the path toward one day becoming North Andover, Massachusetts' "Tire Queen." Every afternoon following her classes at Saint Mary's High School where Sister Elinor Rose taught, Mary cooked for the parish priests at Saint Patrick Parish, earning $1.50 an hour. It wasn't much, but the extra money helped her mother pay the bills. Mary's father had passed away six years earlier, and it was just the two of them living together—her two brothers were a good decade older—in an apartment complex in the working-class city of Lawrence, Massachusetts. Mary had known from a young age that she'd need to support herself.

"Sister Elinor Rose told me Schlott Tire was looking for a file clerk," says Mary, 59. "I told her I didn't want the position. Sister said, 'Too bad, you're taking it. Your interview's tomorrow at 3 p.m. sharp. Don't be late.' Well, I certainly couldn't say no to a nun, so I interviewed and got the position, and my earnings went up to $3 an hour. Looking back, I think Sister was pushing me onto a different path."

Mouse droppings littered the corners of Mary's bare-bones office located next to the tire delivery track. It was loud, cool in the winter, and stuffy in the summer. But Mary liked the people she worked with and was very good at her job. She quickly moved up to accounts receivable. Once, while visiting Schlott's warehouse, Mary picked up a phone that wouldn't stop ringing and made her first sale, a role that would become a regular part of her job description while climbing up the ranks.

Mary enjoyed working for her boss Bill Schlott whom she found to be fair and customer-focused. Once, Bill's son, who was visiting Schlott's retail store, pumped a few quarters into the vending machine to buy a Coke; instead, a beer can rolled out. Turns out the entire vending machine was stocked with beer courtesy of the general manager. On his way out the door, Mary was named his successor.

The problems started with the arrival of a new owner with a very different take on sales and customer service. Shortly after his arrival, Mary had advised a customer that he needed to purchase only three tires for his truck—his spare, she told him, wasn't one of those squishy little donut spares but an actual tire that he could switch out with one of the used tires, which could then serve as the spare. He was grateful for Mary's insights and told her to consider him a regular customer going forward. Mary was pleased; she'd learned early on that word of mouth was the best form of advertising for a small business. Kids she'd known since they were in diapers were now coming to her with their cars. So when the new owner called her into his office, she thought nothing of it. His look said otherwise.

"I heard about what you did today," he said. "So, I'm only going to tell you this once—you cost me money. Going forward, you hit customers once, and you hit them hard. Or you're fired."

It was about to get worse. Rather than appreciating Mary's extensive expertise and camaraderie with old and new customers alike, he viewed her as competition.

"The next time I was called to his office, I was presented with a noncompete agreement, and he pressured me to sign it. I was dumbfounded. So, I asked the owner to hand me the phone. He asked why. 'Because I'm going to call my lawyer,' I told him. Well, he left me alone after that, but I knew what I needed to do—I had never imagined becoming an entrepreneur, but his behavior was the kick in the butt I needed to start my own business."

But there was another problem. Mary didn't have enough money.

Most Popular Ways to Fund a Start-Up   Mary tapped into the three most common ways entrepreneurs fund their start-ups: investing personal funds, fundraising among family and friends, and securing a business loan.

Mary had asked her two older brothers for a loan, and, to her surprise and delight, they were able to scrape together $50,000. Then, a Schlott customer Mary had befriended arranged for her to meet with a bank president in Lowell, Massachusetts, to secure a $50,000 Small Business Association (SBA) loan.

Mary's Independent Tire logo.

SBA loans currently offer many benefits.[1] These include, among others, capped interest rates, long-term financing options, free business counseling, and loan guarantees, which reduces risks for lenders. Challenges entrepreneurs might face when applying for an SBA loan is the need for a healthy credit score, an extensive application process, a slow approval process compared to non-SBA loans, and putting down collateral typically in the form of real estate in the event your business fails. Because SBA loans are financed through individual banks, you may need to shop around. It isn't uncommon to be rejected for lending by one bank but approved by another.

What Mary Did Next   Securing an SBA loan and funding from family along with investing her own hard-earned money was the right move for Mary who, in 1999, launched the aptly named Independent Tire & Auto. She searched for the right location and opted for an affordable storefront in Lawrence, which she later learned didn't have a bathroom. But Mary honored the five-year lease and through the generosity of the owners of a neighboring bar and warehouse had access to their bathrooms. The money she saved over those five years allowed her to pay off both loans. Mary now owned her business outright.

Her hard work and persistence paid off. When Mary cut Independent Tire and Auto's ribbon, most of Schlott's clientele had followed her, eventually leading to Schlott's demise. As her business grew, she found a larger location—with bathrooms—in North Andover, Massachusetts. Local advertising and, most importantly, word of mouth endorsements, grew her clientele even more. For three years in a row, she's earned a spot in the annual Best of Business section in the local *Eagle-Tribune* newspaper.[2]

Sister Elinor Rose would have been proud.

3.3 Fundraising Best Practices

Yes, you're very busy operating your business. But it's only by setting aside dedicated time on your calendar that you'll get into the habit of putting yourself into your investors' shoes. This practice will help you toward your ultimate goal: building a company that is so valuable that someone buys it at a higher price than the original investors valued it.

To better position yourself for success with your various funding sources, we recommend adopting the following best practices.

Family and Friends Fundraising: How to Avoid "Oops, I Lost Your Money" Conversations

Most family members and friends want to support you in following your dreams. Because they aren't typically professional investors, they tend to abide by a "hands-off" approach and are less apt to ask for regular updates on the status of your company.

But often they don't understand how much risk they're taking on by investing in your start-up. If your venture fails, you risk engaging in some very awkward conversations over holiday eggnog. It's imperative to convey to them up front your odds of succeeding and discuss ahead of time what happens if you do indeed fail.

One method of keeping family and friends informed is to create regularly scheduled updates. We recommend at least semi-annually if not quarterly reporting. Here's an example of the topics you may want to address:

- **Opening paragraph:** Convey warmth and build on family bonds by sharing a few personal anecdotes and accomplishments.

- **Overview:** This is a brief snapshot of the state of your business. Briefly share both the positives and the negatives. Now you are ready to get into the specifics.

- **Growth:** How much did your revenue grow, shrink, or stay even? What factors influenced this? If you are in the red, how do you plan to improve? What are your next quarter's projections?

- **Product or service:** If you're creating a product, have there been any further developments or improvements? Are you expanding your services? Improving areas such as functioning and delivery time? What advantages do you have over your competition?

- **People:** Share new hires, advancements, or job openings along with any new goals.

- **Finance:** What's powering your cash flow? Have there been any changes to your financial model? Have you raised more capital or met any financial goals? Be specific.

- **What's next:** What are your goals before the next update? By laying them out, you've created a springboard into your next update.

Grants and Awards: Don't Be Shy, Get the Word Out

Winning grants and awards will help raise the valuation of your company and improve your brand. Be sure to publicize your success in securing them, which may one day help you raise money with professional investors who tend to keep close track of winners as a way of identifying promising new companies. If you opt for a press release, keep it simple and make sure to include the five Ws: who, what, when, where, and why this matters. Then search for and pitch it to the appropriate business publications, post on your website, and adapt key points from your press release for social media posts.

Angel Investors: What They Need to Know

Angel investors—high net-worth individuals or a group of investors who specialize in early-stage financial backing—typically comprehend the level of risk involved and are comfortable taking it on. Unlike taking out a business loan, when you receive funding from an Angel, you're not responsible for paying it back because they will receive equity in your company in exchange for financing. Their hope is that the value of the equity will eventually be larger than the original investment.

Because they tend to be more sophisticated investors, Angels often require investor-friendly terms, so it's important to understand them. Angels are typically successful operators with great networks, so make sure to leverage those networks to recruit management team members, customers, and other investors. And even if an Angel ends up acquiring only a small ownership position in your company, always be respectful of their time. Ignoring their requests for meetings or updates about your company is a bad idea and may negatively resonate throughout your entire network.

Use the family and friends update template to keep Angels informed (we recommend nothing less than quarterly) with an emphasis on the following:

- **Customer retention metrics:** Include the percentage of customers who renew their contracts and the percentage that have declined to renew, and why. Do not obfuscate this.

- **Marketing:** Provide an update on marketing impact, including lead generation results, major press releases, and examples of earned media.

- **Partnerships:** Detail any new partnerships your company has secured or is pursuing. If helpful, ask your investors for contacts with their partnership companies.

- **Ask Angels for help when needed:** Angels know your job is hard and that all start-ups benefit from support and guidance. They want you to succeed—that's why they've invested in you!

Courting Venture Capitalists

Venture capitalists bring value to their founders by writing large checks; helping you recruit a strong management team; and introducing you to early adopter customers, other investors, independent board members, and strategic acquirers. They understand the various stages of a company's growth and are poised to help you navigate complex and tricky situations.

Not all companies, however, are a good fit for venture capital. For instance, "lifestyle" businesses simply don't produce a high enough rate of return for venture investors. But if you believe your company can grow its sales very rapidly and has the potential to go public, venture capital may be an option worth pursuing.

Do your research in identifying and working with a reputable VC firm that best matches your needs with partners you like and trust. Then start building a relationship.

We spoke with Lily Lyman, a partner at Underscore VC and a seasoned founder, investor, and operator in the technology sector, about the most effective ways to approach venture capital firms. According to Lily, one of the most common mistakes founders make is trying to raise money before developing an investor relationship. Most venture firms require more than one partner to approve an investment, so it's important to meet and get to know multiple partners at a single firm and understand who will be the best fit for your specific business.

"It takes time to build strong investor relationships, but once you do they tend to last a long time," says Lily. "In fact, the average founder–investor relationship, which lasts around seven to 10 years,[3] is longer than the *average marriage* in the United States.[4] So, you need to 'date' first instead of aiming for a 'shotgun wedding.'"

Lily stresses to make sure to do your homework on the investor you aim to approach. "I can't tell you how many times I've gotten inbound requests for meetings from a founder running a B2C company, when I only do B2B investing. It's imperative to know what type and at what stage venture firms invest in start-ups," she says.

Once an investment firm has invested in you, it's paramount to keep them updated. "Ideally, engage them as strategic partners; in best cases, they serve as an extension of your team," says Lily. "Keeping investors in the dark is a missed opportunity to build trust and gain strategic value from them. To develop a happy 'marriage' with investors, you need to approach it in a manner similar to that of developing successful relationships in your personal life."

More VC Know-How: Invest in the Same Class of Stock

Know that when raising venture capital for the first time, you'll face a steep learning curve. Be sure to find a mentor or hire a lawyer who can help you interpret a term sheet, which is a document that lays out the conditions and agreements of the venture investments between your early-stage company and the venture firm. There will be many confusing terms and concepts, and you'll need to protect yourself from signing terms that aren't to your benefit.

When raising a round of funding, invest some of your own money into the deal so you are invested alongside the venture capitalists. Do this for each round of funding, and be sure you invest in the same class of stock. Owning the same class of stock as your investors ensures you will receive the same investment terms.

At some point, you may need to share bad news. So many founders are afraid to do so for fear that investors will be angered. It is only by sharing bad news that your investment partners can work to help you remedy the situation.

Be Aware. As part of the terms of their investment, venture capitalists will require that companies provide detailed financial reports using a standard update form that they will provide. In addition to revenue and expenses, they will likely scrutinize your spending, stock option grants, cash burn, accounts payable, and accounts receivable.

A traditional series A venture investor typically looks to own 20% of a company. Venture investors know there will likely be additional funding needs in order to grow, so they will set aside additional capital to invest in subsequent rounds of investment.

Beware. If a founder maintains a controlling share of the company, there may be disagreements with VCs on how to run it, how fast the company should grow, or when to exit the business. But when venture capitalists own as much or more of a company than the founder, they have the ability to remove you and hire a replacement CEO if the company isn't performing to expectations.

Many sales-oriented founders and CEOs are excellent fundraisers. Some are so good at fundraising that they mistakenly believe their company is successful because they've raised a lot of money. This can be a curse. You can never sell too much product, but you can definitely raise too much money and spend too much time doing it at the expense of focusing on growing your core business.

This is where sales and fundraising truly diverge. It is not about how much money a founder raises, but how valuable a business becomes *after* raising the money. A founder wants to raise the maximum amount of capital to make the business successful but not so much money that they significantly dilute their ownership stake.

3.4 What Every Entrepreneur Can Learn from the Challenges of Launching and Growing a Mission-Driven Nonprofit

Fundraising is the lifeblood of mission-driven nonprofits. But while you may find the thought of launching and running a nonprofit rewarding, you will fundamentally be running a business.

To succeed, you'll be tasked with the same challenges facing for-profit businesses: identifying a pain point, devoting energy to maintaining and growing relationships, hiring and managing staff, creating a marketing campaign that conveys a fresh and innovative approach to problem-solving, differentiating your organization from those with similar offerings, and creating a sustainable revenue stream.

Unfortunately, too many nonprofit leaders fail to make this connection, and it shows. According to the National Center on

Charitable Statistics, 30% of nonprofits fail within the first 10 years.[5] And many of those still standing are run inefficiently. So, how do you defy the odds?

Debunking Common Nonprofit Myths and Embracing Best Practices

You are passionate about a cause. Founding a nonprofit organization to solve a problem feels like the next natural step. What better way to support yourself while making a positive impact on the world? Your passion and commitment matters, but it isn't enough.

We spoke with Elise Bates, co-founder and board member of Attane Health, a social enterprise, and the nonprofit End Allergies Together (EAT), which she was inspired to launch to find a cure for food allergies after her daughter experienced a life-threatening reaction to a trace allergen.

Elise shared with us four persistent myths behind running a nonprofit—in particular, a public charity:

#Myth 1: The nonprofit world is collaborative.

Those venturing into the nonprofit sector are often surprised by its competitive nature. In her conversations over the years with leaders running nonprofits and, in particular, public charities, Elise has identified what she calls a "ruthless rivalry," such as competitors stealing donors, advisors, partners, messaging, and URLs. Obviously, not every nonprofit operates in this manner, but be aware that not all organizations with missions similar to yours will exercise a collaborative approach.

Myth #2: Others will care as much as you do.

You assume since you're doing good, others will match your passion. Often, they won't as each person has their own set of priorities. It's up to you to keep employees, board members, and donors motivated and excited about reaching your clearly set and measurable goals.

Myth #3: Those you are supporting will embrace you.

Even the group you're aiding may not embrace your mission with the same amount of passion. For instance, they may not agree with how you portray them in your marketing campaign, or their life situation may not provide the time and energy to involve themselves in pushing your vision forward, even if it's shared. So, understand and listen to the people you aim to help before involving them in your efforts.

Myth #4: Donors affected by the problem you aim to solve will embrace you.

Know that you will be facing *a lot* of competition. While you have identified an important problem to solve, for donors it's another "ask." For your nonprofit to thrive, you must rise above this "asking" noise.

Elise also shared five best practices on running an impactful and financially healthy organization:

Best practice #1: Differentiate yourself.

In 2021, IRS data compiled by Candid counted more than 1.9 million public charities in the United States.[6] While passion may help build your "army," it's important to make a strong business case. Whether you are committed to finding a cure, stemming hunger, or rescuing animals, be as specific as possible about your approach, what you plan to accomplish, the impact of donations and why donors should be involved. By law, nonprofits must publicly post their IRS Form 990[7] to hold them accountable and allow donors to understand their practices and how money is spent. If you spend too much on overhead, you may risk losing their support.

Best practice #2: Make it clear how you measure success.

Donors need to know how you measure success. For instance, does your work aim to impact legislation or public policy? If it's to advance scientific research, how? Science can seem like a black hole, and many donors may wonder if their donation is really going to make a difference. Clearly convey how you measure success—donors need to understand their impact to feel proud about contributing to your cause.

Best practice #3: Storytelling is critical.

People have short attention spans, so keep communications brief and impactful. You can't tell the same story for 10 years no matter how traumatic the event behind the creation of the charity. Continue to deepen the narrative by sharing stories of those impacted by your work. To be self-sustaining, you must continually make the problem behind your cause relevant to donors.

Best practice #4: Tailor your message to different groups.

The same message won't work for everyone. As such, you must translate your vision onto other people's perceptions of the world to engage with them. For example, doctors, patients, parents, friends, restaurants, schools, food companies, and other organizations all have different reasons for wanting to cure food allergies. By better understanding each audience you hope to engage, you are better positioned to launch a strong segment marketing campaign.

Best practice #5: Go into business first.

A well-run organization with limited overhead will be attractive to donors. Working at a for-profit business will allow you to peek under the "hood" and observe what the business is doing well and how you might improve upon operations. When you're ready to transition into founding a nonprofit, find a mentor who can help you navigate your journey and key business decisions. Ultimately, with experience in both the for- and nonprofit sectors, you are better positioned to launch and scale up your own organization.

Case Study on Beating the Odds

Marvin Pierre, whom we'll meet next, is the embodiment of an unlikely entrepreneur who succeeded in launching and scaling a mission-driven nonprofit. Fueled by passion and buoyed up by his hard-earned business skills, Marvin overcame tremendous odds and, in the process, mastered telling his nonprofit's story in a way that continues to resonate with individuals and corporations alike. Every entrepreneur can glean lessons from Marvin's story.

3.5 Marvin Pierre, Founder and Executive Director of Eight Million Stories, Inc.: Disrupting the School-to-Prison Pipeline

Most everyone in Marvin Pierre's South Jamaica neighborhood in Queens, New York, knew Jungle, a homeless man with a flamboyant streak. On Easter Sundays he would don a baby blue suit and wish passersby a happy holiday. Most days he wore a trench coat and boots, sometimes donning a floppy hat if he felt silly. When he was drunk, he would dance. When he was tired, he would lay his blanket out in front of the neighborhood bar or supermarket and sleep. Neighbors loved Jungle and looked out for him. And sometimes, when he was sober, he dropped little pearls of wisdom.

"Stay in school, young man."

A teenage Marvin Pierre passed by Jungle every day on his way to high school. What impacted Marvin most about Jungle's advice was the homeless man's past—not that long ago he'd been a well-respected businessman who wore sharp suits and carried a briefcase instead of pushing around his life's possessions in a shopping cart.

Marvin Pierre, founder of Eight Million Stories.
Photo credit: Killy.

"It's funny how, if you're paying attention, mentors can present themselves in unexpected forms," says Marvin, 41, co-founder and executive director of Eight Million Stories, Inc., a nonprofit that supports underserved youth in Houston in completing their education and obtaining meaningful employment. "Jungle turned out to be part of my life experience, and what he said stayed with me. He made me more determined to find a way out."

Leaving, however, was no easy feat. In the 1920s, after a construction boom, South Jamaica's population swelled with African Americans[8] searching for work, housing, and a better life. As their numbers grew, an exodus of white people followed. By the 1930s, the city was overrun with ramshackle housing and a notable lack of infrastructure.[9] As too many city leaders looked the other way, serious social issues crept in.

In 1966, President Lyndon B. Johnson designated South Jamaica as a poverty zone during the launch of his administration's War on Poverty.[10] The 1960s and 1970s saw a heroin epidemic[11] followed by an influx of crack cocaine in the 1980s,[12] further scarring the neighborhood and fueling the growth and influence of gang activity.

Working-class families like Marvin's whose dad drove a taxi navigated these harsh realities every day. He and Marvin's mother, who was employed as a home attendant, were determined to imprint on Marvin the importance of education in building a better life and escaping the allure of gangs as a second family.

Marvin's way out would take the form of football. It was here on the playing field that he would develop a friendship with a teammate he'd one day join on a car ride that would alter the course of his life.

Tabor Academy The brochure depicted a massive white Tudor-style building with a bell tower perched between a series of slanted red roofs overlooking the sea. "It's called a *prep* school," said Marvin's teammate as they chatted in English class. "My Uncle Joe wants me to go here. We're visiting the campus soon."

"What do you mean you're leaving?" said Marvin. "You can't get rid of me that easily. I'm coming with you."

The school threatening to upend Marvin's friendship was Tabor Academy, an independent preparatory school in Marion, Massachusetts, situated on the shores of Sippican Harbor. The uncle, Joe Marino, was a Tabor alumnus who scouted talent for the Academy through Pop Warner in New York City's often overlooked boroughs with the goal of bringing bright students who were promising players onto Tabor's football team.

They were a group of four that day—Marvin, Joe, his friend, and his friend's father—on the road to the Tabor Academy campus in the spring of 1999. Once there, Marvin was encouraged to interview as well. Both Joe and the Tabor admissions board agreed he'd be a great asset to the school. They would help Marvin secure financial aid so he could enroll at the start of his sophomore year. Ironically, his friend decided not to apply.

Now it was time to convince his parents to endorse the big move. What played out in Marvin's home was a dilemma faced by many parents who strive to create a better life for their children but, at the same time, fear the exposure to a new environment embedded in a social class unlike their own will impact how they relate to one another. "Mom told me to never forget where I came from," recalls Marvin. He couldn't have known at the time, but his mother's advice would shape his future entrepreneurial journey.

Lift as You Climb *This is a high school?*

Marvin was blown away by the newness of Tabor Academy's classroom equipment, a cafeteria with an all-you-can eat policy, freshly painted dorm rooms, small class sizes, and expansive athletic facilities all punctuated by the scent of salt water from the Atlantic Ocean lapping at the campus shoreline. He found himself among new peers being groomed for success where such alumni as Reebok founder and president Paul Fireman, class of '62[13] and Rear Admiral Archer Macy Jr. class of '71,[14] had tread before them. But Marvin's transition to life in this idyllic setting would prove to be much more difficult than he'd imagined.

At his old public school, African American students made up the majority of the student body. Now, Marvin found himself among one of only ten Black students. Nearly everyone at Christ the King High hailed from poor or working-class backgrounds, creating common cultural reference points that now barely existed.

He felt like he was swimming against a current determined to whisk him away.

Then Dr. Sam McFadden stepped up to the plate. He was a local African American resident who supported the school and, in a volunteer capacity, took struggling students under his wing.

"Dr. McFadden was both a mentor and a father figure to me," says Marvin who recalls their shared little moments together like grabbing pizza and wings or cleaning out his garage. During such activities they would talk about Marvin's fears, hopes, and dreams. "Dr. McFadden told me to always remember to pull another person up the ladder as I climbed. And I never forgot that."

Lift as you climb.

An Education in Finance Just as playing football had opened doors for Marvin in South Jamaica, he developed friendships on Tabor's playing field. This led to weekend visits to new friends' homes who lived in the area.

"They had so much more than me," says Marvin. But rather than feeling sorry for himself, these visits evoked curiosity and action. "I asked one friend what his father did for a living, and he said he worked as an investment banker. I decided then and there that one day I'd work in finance, too. His father read the *Wall Street Journal*, so I took to reading it every day."

Marvin received his first real lesson in personal finance from an unlikely mentor. After promoting his availability to do lawn work, he built up a customer base and, at one point, earned $600. He spent it all on new clothes.

"One of my new friends laughed at me and said, 'Marvin, I put my money in the bank. I will always be $600 richer than you for the rest of our lives.' That blew me away and inspired a lifetime of my saving and investing money."

Marvin graduated from Tabor Academy in 2002. Four years later he earned a bachelor's degree in economics from Trinity College. His first post-graduation job? Working on Wall Street as a financial analyst at Goldman Sachs, one of the world's premier investment banking and financial services companies.

Mission accomplished . . . for now.

Low-Number Kids   Two years after accepting his position at Goldman Sachs, a close friend from Tabor Academy invited Marvin to speak at Clinton Hill, a public school in Brooklyn where she taught fifth grade. She hoped Marvin's success story would inspire her students from similar backgrounds. On the day of his presentation, he reviewed the list of students. Next to each name was a number that indicated the student's reading level.

"My gut told me that those students with the lowest numbers were more likely to drop out of school, which would increase their chances of ending up in prison," he said. "Those low numbers haunted me."

Something inside Marvin clicked. Just as he had once been determined to learn how to secure a career in the financial sector, he now wanted to learn what it would take for struggling students like the ones he was about to address to achieve success. And once empowered, what would it take for these students to then empower other kids to be successful? This extra step, he determined, would further close the opportunity gap. Marvin articulated his mission: that of transforming the lives of vulnerable youth through education, skills training, and mentoring relationships like the one he built with Dr. McFadden.

Lift as you climb.

Understanding the Problem After nearly three years of employment at Goldman Sachs, Marvin left in 2009 to accept a position as associate dean of scholar life at Summit Academy Charter School in Brooklyn followed by the role of dean of students at the New York City–based Uncommon School. Both institutes stressed the importance of pairing a supportive environment with academic rigor, which resonated with Marvin. He later transitioned into the role of assistant principal of KIPP Texas Public Schools in Houston where, in his first year, he led the work of transforming an all-boys middle school by changing the culture and reducing school suspensions.

"The incarceration of juvenile youth who lack support and employment prospects upon release results in a struggle to re-enter society and they face a high risk of recidivism, setting them up for a lifelong cycle of poverty and imprisonment. This pattern made me ask: what if disconnected youth who've been pushed out of public school systems had the opportunity to complete their education and obtain meaningful employment in an academic environment that worked for them?"

Marvin embarked on a mission to crush the school-to-prison pipeline that sweeps a disproportionately high number of Houston's Black youth into the criminal justice system by better positioning disconnected students to learn trade and life skills with the goal of securing meaningful employment. In turn, he reasoned that a successful program could influence school districts and the juvenile justice system to invest in alternative pathways for students who don't function as well in traditional school settings.

In 2016, Marvin stepped away from the security of his role as an assistant principal to launch an education center. "I flung myself into the void," he says. "There was no looking back."

Eight Million Stories: Creating an Identity   In 1993, hip-hop group A Tribe Called Quest released a song titled *Eight Million Stories*. In it, Phife Dawg raps about having a really bad day and constantly running into trouble. But he knows he's not alone. He realizes that the thousands of floors of project housing surrounding him are home to millions of struggling people.[15]

"The song's refrain is a cry for help," says Marvin who first listened to A Tribe Called Quest as a teenager in South Jamaica. "There are kids involved in the juvenile justice system who aren't necessarily bad. If you listen closely enough, you realize they're mouthing the same refrain."

Choosing the right name for his start-up turned out to be the easy part. Marvin was about to come face-to-face with the biggest X factor that's taken down both non- and for-profit ventures: raising money.

Eight Million Stories, Inc., was in debt at the start. After Houston's Juvenile Probation Department sent out a request for proposals, Marvin's fiscal sponsor took out a mandatory $70,000 bond as an insurance policy required by Harris County Juvenile Probation in the event that the nonprofit walked away from its contract. Climbing out of debt hinged on Marvin's ability to raise funds. But Marvin had never in his life raised money for a cause. He reflected on his time at Goldman Sachs for inspiration.

"When you work on Wall Street, you understand the importance of building relationships," he says. "I had gained insight into how the private sector works and how to get things done efficiently."

Marvin created his first promotional slide deck on his laptop that encapsulated Eight Million Stories' mission, the problem it aimed to solve, his proposed solutions, and projected outcomes. While he was pleased with his messaging, the deck itself was, in Marvin's own words, "a work in progress." His skills in executing a more polished form of marketing material would grow in tandem with his start-up.

Marvin had never thought of himself as a salesperson, and he didn't have much to sell at that point beyond his mission. So, he approached selling the idea of Eight Millions Stories to potential donors in a manner that worked best for him. "Sales, to me, is about telling a story in a persuasive manner that makes people care," says Marvin. "And I discovered early on that I was a passionate storyteller."

And like anyone "selling" an untested start-up, Marvin experienced plenty of rejection. "Follow up with us once Eight Million Stories begins to reach its goals" became a common refrain.

Marvin understood that potential donors were thinking: *Can I bet on him? Will he quit if the going gets tough?* Undeterred, he continued knocking on the doors of nonprofits and wealthy individuals, building awareness in the process. Eventually he won over his first major donor, an entrepreneur who had created and sold a successful medical company.

"There wasn't yet a building or a curriculum. So, I was essentially 'selling' my mission," says Marvin. "My first donor liked my passion, commitment, and skill set I would bring to the school. He took a bet on me, and I am so appreciative of that."

Growing Pains Marvin applied for and was accepted into an entrepreneurship incubator that offered resources and mentorship to start-ups like his navigating early-stage challenges such as fundraising and market research. He was then accepted into a four-month accelerator program with educational workshops and networking opportunities focused on the next stages of entrepreneurial growth.

"The biggest challenge was juggling all the work involved in launching a start-up with the commitments involved in being part of an incubator and accelerator," says Marvin. "But I highly recommend them."

According to the *Harvard Business Review* article "What Sets Successful Startup Accelerators Apart," start-ups that participated in an accelerator raised 50% to 170% more from investors and were more likely to be "alive" or acquired than similar start-ups that applied to the accelerators but were not accepted.[16]

As he continued to fundraise, Marvin hired three full-time staff members and identified a colleague to run the day-to-day programming. Then he secured a "cottage" to serve as the education center's building.

"Oh my God, what a mess. That cottage was more like a run-down shack," recalls Marvin. "Everything about it was old, dirty, and dingy. Talk about humble beginnings." Marvin and his staff began the tedious process of rehabbing the building along with purchasing computers, supplies, and affordable, mismatched furniture.

Students were referred to Eight Million Stories by case managers and juvenile probation officers with a focus on those struggling to earn or ambivalent about earning a high school degree. The most underperforming public schools in the Houston area received highest priority. Marvin was determined that every student who graduated from Eight Million Stories would earn a GED.

Forty students made up the first class. "They were tough inner-city kids from broken homes, scarred by the social issues they were born into," says Marvin. "Those early years of adaptation were challenging on both sides. More than once our schoolhouse was broken into, and all our computers were stolen."

There were other growing pains along the way. "We'd advertised that we would pay our students to attend classes where they'd learn a trade," says Marvin. "Turns out we were too inexperienced in properly executing the plan, and the costs exceeded our funds. In short, we over-promised and under-delivered. After the first month, we had to break the news to students and parents that this approach was unsustainable."

Eight Million Stories' student body immediately dropped down from forty kids to only 6.

Marvin also learned a valuable lesson in hiring and managing staff. "Some people are very good at interviewing; they say all the right things. But then their skills and performance don't match their words. I've become better at analyzing and getting interviewees to talk about their skill sets. And I've learned to pay attention to the unscripted moments in the interview process to better gauge the whole person."

Was there a bright side to all of this? "My coping skills improved," says Marvin. "I'm much less rattled now when facing setbacks."

Betting the House   Nothing speaks more about academic success than a student who graduates from college and secures a professional job. If Marvin could help one of his students achieve this goal, he reasoned their success story would attract more donors.

On the surface, Briana was an unlikely candidate. As a child, she'd known homelessness and spent her formative years living in a shelter. Her school record was plagued with truancy, and during her teenage years her family had disowned her. But Marvin recognized in her an ambition fueled by resiliency. Briana proved to be a smart and talented student and, through Eight Million Stories, earned her GED. Like Marvin before her, she wanted to major in business.

Thanks to his own informal lesson in finance from his friend at Tabor Academy, Marvin had never spent his $10,000 signing bonus from Goldman Sachs. With the costs incurred from launching and growing the school, he had around $25,000 left in the bank. That was it. Now, Marvin was about to risk it all.

"I told Briana I was going to pay her college tuition that scholarships didn't cover," says Marvin. "In return, I stressed the importance of her graduating, for herself and for Eight Million Stories' future. The school's future, and mine, were tied to her ability to do so."

Briana was accepted into the business program at Southern University at New Orleans, a historically Black public college with politicians and education leaders among their alumni. Marvin rolled the dice.

His "return on investment" was more than he could have hoped for. True to her word, Briana made the Dean's List every year. During the summer she interned with Eight Million Stories, gaining experience in the business of running a nonprofit. And Marvin wasn't the only one who recognized her academic talents: Southern University named Briana "Miss College of Business," and she served as a representative for the business school culminating in a parade where she waved to the crowds lining the streets from a float created by the school. She proudly took Marvin on a tour of her campus.

"Briana's success reminded me why I got into this," says Marvin. "Lifting as you climb is truly the most satisfying feeling."

Eight Million Stories Matures   Marvin takes great pride in the fact that all 62 students who have graduated from Eight Million Stories have earned their GED. And like Briana before them, seven students are currently enrolled in or have gone on to graduate from college. Currently, 70 students make up Eight Million Stories' student body.

Marvin's fundraising deck has matured along with his sales presentation, which remains grounded in storytelling. National brands are now among those who have donated to Eight Million Stories.

Marvin said goodbye to the schoolhouse cottage a few years back after taking over a contract for a high school building in the district. He and his staff—which has grown from three full-time employees to twelve—are busy renovating it. He is currently pursuing a housing component so students outside of Houston's public transportation system will have the opportunity to enroll as well.

Marvin's ties to Tabor Academy, where he now serves on the board of trustees, remains strong. And as for Eight Million Stories being $80,000 in the hole, Marvin is proud to report that they've climbed out.

Early on, Marvin's biggest fear was not being able to raise enough money and failing to pay people's salaries. But rather than being overwhelmed by fear, he converted it into motivation. "Fundraising can be really challenging year after year," says Marvin. "It tends to be cyclical, with some donors falling off while new donors who want to see progress, growth, and impact are cultivated. When a down cycle hits, as they sometimes do, some leadership lose motivation. I say don't waver from your convictions."

To date, Marvin has never employed a fundraising specialist or marketer. "It's all me. You need to be willing to step out of your comfort zone and get out there and pitch, which is why I'm still here. I surprised myself by how much I enjoy the challenge."

Marivin's vision is a future where outcomes for youth are no longer predictable by skin color, ZIP code, or income. He's remaining true to this mission one story at a time.

4

Leadership

The Sled Only Moves as Fast as the Lead Dog

4.1 Avoid Becoming a "Flailing Founder"

In launching a start-up and building a winning team, it's crucial for a scrappy entrepreneur to oversee the details of every business decision. Making those initial hires, signing first customers, raising money, and growing the start-up is more than a full-time job—it's a matter of survival where the stakes could not be any higher. Failing on any of these fronts often means bankruptcy.

But a company with humble beginnings—Lou once worked for a start-up with two employees, a shedding dog, and three broken vacuum cleaners—and the intensely focused and uncompromising founder behind its rise must evolve as the company grows larger and its needs become more complex. Founders will be tasked with transitioning from the overseer of day-to-day functions to delegating to a management team the tasks of running a company at scale. Successfully running a start-up in survival mode is no longer a superpower.

Easier said than done. It's hard to step back and hand the reins over to managers who may approach their responsibilities in a manner different from your own. But a lack of trust in one's management team and an inability to empower them in the decision-making process is a recipe for micromanaging a company to its death.

At this stage, it's not uncommon for a company to outgrow its founder.

Signs of a Flailing Founder come in many forms. Consistently missing sales forecasts and product release dates, losing large customers, and the resignation of senior management team members point to founders in over their heads. If improvements aren't made, there comes a point when it's clear to investors that the founder needs to be removed from the leadership helm to prevent the company from failing.

The Flailing Founder phenomenon is evident in the many ongoing CEO searches in the marketplace at any given time. As we are writing this book, there are one dozen CEO searches open for Boston companies bringing in between $50 million to $200 million in sales. In most cases, it's because the founder hasn't been able to take the company to the next level.

Thus, as a company grows, executive leadership becomes the founder's most important skill.

In 1983, while playing for the Harvard Crimson's men's ice hockey team, Mark Fusco was the first ever defenseman to receive the Hobey Baker Award.

Photo credit: Harvard University.

4.2 Lessons on Leadership: Mark Fusco, Olympic Athlete and CEO

Don't pay employees to work hard—pay them to win. This, according to Mark Fusco, is the difference between managing and leading.

Mark, 64, is a U.S. Hockey Hall of Fame inductee[1] who, in his role as CEO and president of Aspen Technology, turned the struggling provider of software and services for the process industries into a powerhouse. When Mark was named CEO in 2005, the company's stock was priced at $4.50 with a market capitalization of $400 million. By the end of 2013 when Mark retired, the stock price had jumped to $35 per share with a market capitalization of more than $3 billion. He credits his philosophy on leadership as the guiding force in his creation of $2.6 billion in enterprise value during his tenure.

"Theoretically, working hard should translate into creating value for your company, shareholders, and customers," says Mark. "But if your company isn't organized around a shared goal, you will lack alignment and purpose and end up overinvesting in some areas and underinvesting in others."

Building a winning team, Mark stresses, starts with the founder. "The sled only goes as fast as the lead dog. Everyone in an organization knows the pace the CEO sets, so if the CEO isn't the first in the office and the last to leave, it sends a signal."

But leading by example alone is not enough. "In both business and hockey, it's the leader with the best team who ultimately wins."

Leadership on the Ice   Mark Fusco's earliest lessons in leadership took place in the backyard of his childhood home in Burlington, Massachusetts, which his father flooded during cold winter months to create a makeshift skating rink. It was here that he and his brother Scott honed their skills playing neighborhood pickup games. In 1983, while playing for the Harvard Crimson's men's ice hockey team, Mark was the first ever defenseman to receive the Hobey Baker Award,[2] an honor given annually to the best collegiate hockey player in the United States. He took his passion for hockey to the next level one year later by earning a spot on the U.S. Olympic Men's Ice Hockey team followed by a two-year career playing professionally with the NHL's Hartford Whalers.

"Hockey moves very quickly and, as a player, you need to train yourself to see the other nine skaters simultaneously while calculating where and how quickly they're moving and with what intent," says Mark. "I would visualize plays and movements over and over in my head because when it came time to execute them, there was no time to think—I had to act immediately in order to control the puck. Breaking left or right potentially changes the outcome of the game."

Similarly, business runs in cycles and sequences, and certain outcomes manifest weekly, monthly, and quarterly. "In both business and sports, you need a shared vision of how teams work and what you need to do to win."

The Sports and Adversity Leadership Edge Mark's assertion that playing on a sports team builds leadership skills and gives CEOs an edge is backed by research. For example, in a 2023 study conducted by Deloitte,[3] 91% of surveyed women in leadership roles said the skills they developed through playing sports were important to succeeding in their professional careers.

"Athletic intensity can be channeled into mastering the skills needed to win in business," says Mark. "Both are competitive in nature, and success comes down to execution."

But what if you've never had the opportunity to play on a sports team or athletics simply doesn't interest you?

"Apply the lessons you've learned in facing adversity," says Mark. "You may not realize you have a leadership toolkit at your disposal."

Think of the times you've bumped up against your limitations. If you revisit those painful situations through the lens of skills gained and lessons learned, you realize how those life events forced you to change. You now have hard-earned experience in such areas as crisis management, risk taking, building resilience, learning to accept limitations, and strategic thinking. You've built character, which is essential for effective leadership.

Even a painful job loss, so difficult to process at the time, might be what it takes to set you on your entrepreneurial journey.

Putting Out a Dumpster Fire   In 2005, three months into his role as CEO, Mark was in the midst of discovering just how extensive Aspen Technology's problems really were. After the company went public in 1994, the leadership team went on a buying spree and made 23 acquisitions across 13 countries, creating 19 different software development centers around the globe.[4] Aspen Technology embodied the classic mistake of growing too big too fast, a move that ultimately spread the management team thin. As cloud computing grew, it became clear to Mark that their pricing model, which relied on perpetual licenses and annual software maintenance, needed to change as the industry moved to subscription-based pricing. Some team members weren't pulling their weight and would need to be let go. And just as Mark was trying to correct Aspen Technology's financial woes, a class-action lawsuit was filed against the company in response to former leaderships' issuance of misleading statements and improper revenue recognition. Radical changes were needed to right the ship.

Mark forged ahead. He recruited a new management team, redesigned the company's pricing model to unlock both customer satisfaction and better profit margins, consolidated the 19 remote software development sites down to three, and focused his attention on growth and profitability. His persistence and grit paid off, creating $2.6 billion in enterprise value for the company during his tenure.

More Guiding Leadership Principles for Entrepreneurs

Marks' approach to leadership played a vital role in Aspen Technology's turnaround. Here are more guiding principles he shared with us, which are applicable at any stage of your company's evolution:

Check your ego at the door: Looking in the mirror and seeing greatness has nothing to do with hiring the best people. There is strength in being humble and in learning from people who are smarter than you. When you look beyond yourself, you gain greater insight into how to assemble all the components of a company so that they work together more effectively.

Do what you need to do within the rules of the game: I don't agree with the stereotype of the cutthroat CEO. Ruthlessness and a lack of morals don't pay off in the long run. The most effective CEOs are trustworthy and engaged in running their companies to the best of their abilities. There's a reason why referees are vital to sports.

We all lack self-awareness at a certain point: You are in a leadership position for a reason. Ask yourself—how did you get here? Amplify what you're good at, hone necessary skills, and don't directly take on what you're not good at. It's that simple.

Consistency versus overachieving: In sports you must be consistent every single time you play. Similarly, on Wall Street you don't get paid to overachieve. During one quarter if you overachieve by 25% but then underachieve by 5% the next, you're penalized. To achieve excellence, aim for a consistent performance.

Overcome your inclination to micro-manage: Great leaders understand that the success of the company cannot rely solely on them. Recognize that dealing with day-to-day demands takes you away from the big picture and the strategies you must develop to get there. You need a great team to both scale the company and rely on their ability to help attract and retain exceptional talent.

Lead through action, not just through words: Many companies are evaluated on their quarterly sales results. A successful leader can't skip out during key periods and expect employees to remain engaged. If your team is making sales calls, so do you. You need to be first in and the last out—that's your obligation. The message you convey is that we're all in this together.

Articulate clear goals: You can't create a roadmap without goal posts. If your vision isn't conveyed clearly, it's more challenging to measure or reward employee accomplishments.

Set up employees for success: A key role in a CEO's job is putting teams of employees in a position to work together successfully. If a decision succeeds, give credit to the employees behind it. If a decision fails, share the responsibility with them. Because support builds trust. And when employees win, the company wins.

Root out low performers: There's often a misconception that an employee with a questionable performance is going to improve. People are who they are. It's only by assembling the best team possible that you can make significant progress in growing your business.

Recognize that not every employee needs to be a superstar: I own horses and I love them, but they're not running in the Kentucky Derby. Likewise, not everyone on your team will become high performers. Realize it's not your job to make everyone a superstar; your job is to assemble a great team with both high-achievers and role players.

When interviewing a candidate, encourage storytelling: If I'm interviewing a candidate, I get them to tell me a story because I'm trying to understand who they are beyond their résumé. Recognize, too, that truly successful people won't feel the need to brag about what they've achieved.

Don't forget about family: Work can be all-consuming, so you must prioritize your family relationships. A balanced life equals balanced leadership.

4.3 Why Distributed Leadership Works

For strategic planning purposes, it's standard practice for companies to create five- to ten-year business plans. But while it's essential to set growth targets and flesh out a long-term vision, even the best-laid plans may not be enough to protect your company when life hurls curveballs your way in the form of cyberattacks, pandemics, disruptions to supply chains, natural disasters, or geopolitical conflicts, among others. As your company grows, you will benefit from instituting a distributed leadership model to nurture a strategic, flexible, and agile workforce that is better positioned to respond to and mitigate crises.

Key military victories illustrate the effectiveness of distributed leadership. In the early 1800s, when European armies functioned as large, single entities with no substructure higher than the regiment,[5] Napoleon Bonaparte revolutionized the battlefield by dividing his army into smaller divisions of 20,000 to 40,000 soldiers.[6] Commanded by individual marshals, these "mini-armies" were capable of great speed, flexibility, and independent deployment. With a shorter chain of command, Napoleon's corps could seamlessly pivot without undue confusion. Centralizing his "mission command" while decentralizing his marshals' decision-making process set the stage for Napoleon to win 53 out of 60 major battles.[7]

During the Civil War, General Ulysses S. Grant took his interpretation of mission command a step further by creating within his army what he called a "thinking machine"[8]—a culture based on trust in which local commanders could take risks without fear of retribution in the event that they failed.

Deborah Ancona, a professor of organization studies and founder of the MIT Leadership Center at MIT Sloan, has written extensively about the need for companies to shift from a reliance on command-and-control leadership to distributed leadership, which she defines as collaborative, autonomous practices managed by a network of formal and informal leaders across an organization.

In an article published in MIT Sloan's *Ideas Made to Matter*,[9] she and co-author Kate Isaacs, a senior lecturer at MIT Sloan, share insights on how companies can adopt a distributed leadership model:

- When people at lower levels of the firm have ideas on new strategic objectives that have been vetted and tested, let those people participate in leading the change process.

- Give people a say in matching themselves with roles. Engage in two-way dialogue with potential candidates to consider who has the passion, knowledge, networks, and time availability to succeed—regardless of a person's role or level in an organizational hierarchy.

- Have honest conversations with potential team members about their capacity to implement and what they can commit to the team.

- Provide coaching and learning opportunities so that people can practice the decision-making, entrepreneurial activity, and influencing skills needed to work in this mode of operating. Provide opportunities for employees to meet one another and network across the firm.

Transitioning from command-and-control doesn't mean senior leaders won't play a role in the process. Prof. Ancona likens them to architects whose focus is facilitating and enabling entrepreneurial activity within the company.

Ultimately, by creating a culture that tolerates failure, you win.

4.4 A Test in Leadership: Entrepreneurship Through Acquisition (ETA)

What if you yearn to become an entrepreneur but feel overwhelmed by the thought of building a company from scratch, finding your first customers, hiring a team, and financing the business? What if, despite your desire to be your own boss, creating something out of nothing feels like too big of a risk?

ETA, also known as search funds, is an increasingly popular way to become an entrepreneur by buying an existing business. Acquiring a company is a lower-risk endeavor than launching a start-up since an existing business has already achieved product/market fit, has an established customer base, and a management team in place. In fact, the 2024 Stanford Graduate School of Business Search Fund Study found that nearly seven in ten acquired companies generated positive returns.[10]

Rob Ketterson, founding partner of the growth equity firm Volition Capital, agrees. "The mortality rate for most search fund deals is under 10%, whereas in the start-up world it is closer to 90%." Ketterson points out that overall search fund companies have a bigger economic impact than start-ups. "Search fund companies that grow from $3 million in sales to $30 million create more jobs and have a bigger impact on the economy than a start-up that goes from $0 to $3 million in revenue."

Entrepreneurs seeking to acquire a company—called *searchers*—should first identify the industry niche in which they want to operate. Then the search for an available business to purchase kicks off. Typical search methods include cold calls, email blasts, LinkedIn messages, or hiring the services of a broker specializing in ETA who can source potential companies to buy.

You'll need to raise capital before approaching interested business owners or those you hope to convince to sell. While search times may vary, we recommend giving yourself at least one year with the knowledge that in some cases it might take longer.

As the new owner of an existing business, you may have ideas for modernizing your acquired company's operations. You may have a new vision in mind for your company and the steps necessary to achieve your goals. But you're about to grapple with a built-in ETA challenge: you've inherited a workforce used to functioning in a certain way that may be resistant to change.

Thus, leadership plays one of the most important roles in succeeding in ETA. Just ask two search finders who took on big leadership challenges on their way to turning profits.

Mason Barrett, HurtVet: Rising to the Challenges of ETA Leadership

For Mason Barrett, ETA was a no-brainer.

"Acquiring a successful company and taking it to the next level was more attractive to me than building a business from the ground up," says Mason. "It's how I'm wired."

Key factors in Mason's search were a company's insulation from business cyclicality, levels of recurring revenue, number of years in operation, and proof of product market fit. He wanted to purchase a smaller, steady business he could grow sustainably over time versus one poised for hyper-explosive growth. Of particular interest was acquiring a business from a fellow veteran.

In 2012, after earning his undergraduate degree from Duke University, Mason attended Officer Candidate School to commission as an Ensign in the U.S. Navy. He was a recipient of the OCS Honor Graduate award and had ranked number one in his graduating class of approximately 90 naval officers. After earning his commission, Mason accepted the biggest challenge of his life: training to become a Navy SEAL Officer.

Navy SEAL training, also known as Basic Underwater Demolition/SEAL (BUD/S), is a grueling 24-week program that encompasses physical conditioning, combat dive training, and land warfare. On average, only around 20–25 percent[11] of Navy SEAL candidates make it through all three phases. Following an injury, Mason was among the majority who did not complete the high-risk, high-attrition training program.

"I have no regrets," says Mason. "I had the privilege of leading a small team of enlisted sailors, pushing my limits, and pursuing a dream. I have so much respect for those who succeed and go on to serve in the Naval Special Warfare community along with those who give it their all in training but ultimately have to find another path."

A few years later, while pursuing his MBA at HBS, Mason enrolled in a class on ETA and was hooked. "I hadn't envisioned becoming an entrepreneur, but ETA opened my eyes to the possibility." Following graduation, he founded 360 Bridge LLC, a self-funded search fund, to acquire a veteran-owned small or medium-sized business.

Comfortable functioning in extremes, Mason pushed himself further than most in his pursuit to find a business that checked off all his boxes by researching more than 8,000 companies over an 18-month period. His persistence paid off when he discovered HurtVet Subcontracting, a service-disabled, veteran-owned small business focused on fire, life safety, and security services for the federal government and the U.S. military. After negotiating a purchase agreement, he was the president of his own company.

What Mason hadn't expected was a first year fraught with leadership challenges.

Reflections on Managing a Challenging Employee   One of the first actions Mason took was to embark on a listening tour to better understand the company's strengths and challenges to build trust and develop a knowledge base. Unfortunately for Mason, the former owner's "number two" hadn't learned about the transaction until a general announcement was made.

"I learned that this employee felt betrayed and blindsided. I imagine he must have felt frustrated at having a new boss who was the same age as his children. I dealt with it by being patient and understanding. I gave him my trust. Sadly, it wasn't enough."

The former number two proceeded to act outside of his level of authority, made technical mistakes, and took frustrations out on his colleagues. When Mason presented him with a formal performance improvement plan, the employee quit in a dramatic fashion but not before stealing company trade secrets and conspiring with a direct competitor to divert key contracts and poach employees.

"I became the plaintiff in a civil suit that ran the gamut of our legal system," says Mason. "Even though we won in the end, it was a painful way to learn a lesson."

On the upside, the business has grown and flourished under Mason's leadership. Previously, nearly every consequential decision needed to be approved by the former owner, which created a bottleneck. To remedy this, Mason introduced various levels of delegated managerial authority. "I told my team that up to a certain dollar amount, I trusted them as experts in their areas to make their own decisions. Folks rose to the challenge and responded very positively. Being empowered really helped some employees thrive, and they were able to take on more meaningful roles in the company."

While Mason's evolution in his leadership journey has taught him the importance of empowering and trusting employees, he stresses that leaders can't be afraid to have hard conversations. "It's on the leader to create an environment where difficult conversations can lead to resolution and growth," says Mason.

Revenue has grown by 50% since the acquisition. Mason has spearheaded the expansion of its service offerings and has formalized new partnerships and distributorships. A particular point of pride has been the expansion of the company's 401(k) profit sharing contributions and health insurance benefits. For three years in a row, HurtVet has earned the Department of Labor's platinum-level award in recognition of its commitment to veteran hiring, retention, and professional development.[12]

In light of his experience with former employee number two, Mason continues to play a key role in the hiring of staff. He credits the guidance of advisors and mentors and the adaptation of various hiring theories in the creation of his company's new hiring framework.

"We focus on the experience-based side of the interview that spotlights a candidate's past results. We ask, 'What was at stake, how did you approach it, and how was the situation resolved?'" Most important to Mason is a candidate's character, ethics, and integrity.

Carl Mönefors, Unlikely Lumberjack Manager

In March 2024, Carl Mönefors, 29, traded in his business suit, tie, and tinted sunglasses for hiking clothes as he and his business partner Gabriel Sjöström drove deep into the Swedish forest of Mälardalen to meet with 50 lumberjacks dispersed in groups of three throughout the large, wooded area. The mercury in the central region of Sweden had dipped below the freezing mark. Fighting jet lag, Carl pulled up his collar as he stepped out of the car.

The first group of lumberjacks they encountered were Lithuanian, an ethnic group from one of the three Baltic countries who made up 20 percent of the Naturskog workforce. Carl, unfamiliar with the language, tried to introduce himself and explain that he and his colleague had acquired Naturskog and were the new owners. Carl would be working a good percentage of his time at the various sites in Mälardalen and the adjoining forest of Dalarna, so they'd be seeing him around.

He wasn't sure how much they understood. Then the largest of the three stepped forward and looked Carl up and down. In broken Swedish he said, "Hello, I quit. And the others are coming with me."

The tense encounter would come to define Carl's leadership challenge—building trust among the lumberjacks who were so unlike himself.

An Industry Ripe for Innovation   ETA hadn't originally been part of Carl's business plan. A native of Stockholm, Carl enrolled in entrepreneurship courses at HBS in 2022 in pursuit of the freedom and upside growth potential he believed owning his own business would provide. But as he delved deeper into the discovery process, Carl discerned that his vision of building a venture-backed, global polyester textiles recycling company from the ground up would demand prohibitively high levels of capital investment to fund the building of the factories and infrastructure critical for success.

That's when Carl discovered the ETA pathway to entrepreneurship through HBS courses and insights from the business school's larger entrepreneurial community. Acquiring a company rather than building one from scratch felt like the more practical and strategic move. He partnered with Sjöström, a fellow MBA, and in the summer of 2023 they created an investment company they named Antilop Group with the goal of acquiring multiple Swedish companies. By focusing on Sweden, they felt they held two advantages: because ETA wasn't an established practice in Sweden, there was a whitespace among smaller, well-run companies without clear exit options. In addition, detailed business information on all Swedish companies—including their full profit and loss statements since inception, balance sheets, and data on management, owners, and board members—are publicly accessible.

They narrowed their list down from 10,000 to 500 companies in fields where they respectively held expertise. Among them was forestry and bio-residuals, an industry that was of particular interest to Carl. With nearly 70 percent of Sweden covered by forests and approximately 499 million seedlings planted annually, Sweden's forestry industry was thriving.[13] The country is one of the world's largest exporters of pulp, paper, and sawn timber.[14]

Bio-residuals are the "biological waste" produced from forestry work, which Carl and his colleague planned to process and turn it into biofuels. Sweden currently has one of the highest usages of renewable biofuels in all of Europe.[15]

"I was attracted to forestry because the industry's ripe for disruption," says Carl, who adds that he feels strongly about being part of Sweden's commitment to its green energy transition.

Among Antilop Group's first three acquisitions was Naturskog, an operator of forest management and nature conservation services for public and private landowners. Its core mission was that of promoting sustainable forestry.

Listening and Learning   As Carl prepared to visit Naturskog's sites for the first time in Sweden's Mälardalen and Dalarna forests, he realized he faced three barriers in his new role as a manager of lumberjacks—his young age, his lack of experience in the field of forestry, and his white-collar background.

"I was worried they'd think I was just some finance guy with a fancy education wanting to make money off their labor," says Carl. "I kept thinking, *They've been doing this work for years—why would they listen to me?*"

Fortunately, as Carl traversed the various forest sites during his first on-site visit, the other 47 lumberjacks he met stayed on the job after he made it clear that no one was being fired. He eventually learned that the three Lithuanians had been dissatisfied with the work conditions and hadn't understood that Carl and his colleague had bought the business.

But the Lithuanian workers brought up a good point—work conditions did need to be improved. Under Naturskog's former leadership, the company had grown too fast, and the proper processes and structures weren't put in place for sustained growth. For instance, a group of lumberjacks were given instructions to show up at a new forest site; upon arrival, they discovered that the road was out of commission.

Carl realized he couldn't walk in with all the answers—only questions. "I knew I first had to earn their trust rather than expecting it. So I started by listening."

Listening was harder than it sounded. It meant asking real questions instead of just checking off a box to better understand a world different from his own. It meant standing in the cold during early-morning safety briefings, sitting quietly in break rooms, and showing genuine interest in the work itself.

Gradually, the conversations shifted. Wary glances became nods. Short replies turned into real exchanges. Carl showed he respected the lumberjacks' world enough to step into it. In the process, he was better able to identify problems he could address.

"By introducing solutions to issues the crews were facing in their day-to-day work, I built trust and credibility," he says.

Of greatest value to Carl was working in the field. He initially traveled a lot with his management team to different forestry sites to understand where further improvements could be made. Carl currently spends 80 percent of his time on operations and 20 percent working in the office on the mergers and acquisitions agenda. "I learned so much more by working directly with the teams of lumberjacks than I would have if I'd studied PowerPoint charts in an office."

Carl's approach has paid off. Naturskog was generating $12 million in annual revenue when Antilop acquired the company in 2024. In just one year they have more than doubled in size, driven in part by a combination of successful geographic expansion initiatives and add-on acquisitions.

As for what's next for Carl, he's shared with us that he's proudly earning a chainsaw certificate.

Tell Me About a Time . . . Tips on Interviewing Candidates

As Mason discovered, there isn't a one-size-fits all approach to hiring. "While a candidate's skill set is important, their lived work experience and ability to fit into the company's culture takes precedence," says Michelle Goodwin, a seasoned senior human resources professional with more than 25 years of experience working at fast-paced, high-growth technology companies. "I start by looking at what a candidate has accomplished and ask open-ended questions such as 'Can you tell me about a time . . .?' You'll learn a lot about a candidate this way. *Then* we move onto their skillset."

Michelle recommends an employee probation period of at least 90 days and no more than six months. "It's within this time period that you'll be able to tell if the employee is a good fit. With senior-level employees, six months provides an accurate window into their performance and potential."

Beyond this time frame, "you should trust your gut," says Michelle. "A senior-level employee who started out strong may improve a faltering performance with coaching. Others may still struggle even with that extra support. If this is the case, you need to cut your losses quickly to cause the least amount of disruption to the team."

For merit-based compensation, Michelle's HR team uses a "bell curve" to categorize employees based on performance to make sure high-performers are rewarded. At one company where she worked, managers were giving all their reports five on a five-point rating scale. "Of course we want to think every employee is a rock star, but we need to be realistic to make performance-based recognition really count," she says.

At her current workplace, Michelle runs employee and manager training a few times a year. With a focus on exploring training techniques, teaching employees how to use tools to grow and develop their careers, and sharing coaching techniques, she provides tools managers can offer their direct reports.

Tips for Start-up Hiring: Transparency Is Crucial If you are still laying down the foundation on which to build your winning team, it's particularly important to recognize that in an early-stage start-up employees will be playing multiple roles in an ever-evolving environment. As such, not every candidate will function well in the start-up space, says Michelle.

"Unlike an established business, start-up culture is often fueled by rapid growth, risk taking, and disrupting markets," says Michelle. "As such, you need employees who are nimble and quick to adapt to changes in the marketplace. They must enjoy taking on challenges."

Michelle once worked at a start-up that was scaling like crazy, and at one point the chief financial officer (*CFO*) hired 25 new people. But he couldn't understand why, over a short period of time, the employees were quitting. "It turns out the CFO painted a rosy picture of what it was like to work at the company," says Michelle. "This didn't convey the reality of our culture during a period of intense growth."

Rather than embracing a "hire anybody" approach—Michelle once worked with a founder who hired his first round of employees off Craigslist—she advocates for transparency. "If you want to attract employees who thrive in this sort of environment, you need to be honest and convey the challenges up front. Yes, you're going to work long and hard over the next few years as the company matures. And you'll either benefit from growing with the company or you'll make an impact within that time period that'll look great on your résumé."

In a company's early stages, Michelle notes that employees typically won't find the type of systems and processes that are commonly in place at mature companies, and they'll need to be comfortable with the lack of structure. "I once grew a company from 40 employees to 400 using only Excel spreadsheets before we invested in more sophisticated software," says Michelle.

As your start-up matures, you need to adopt a more thoughtful and selective process, followed by the company investing in those employees who show promise. One way to attract, retain, and grow a talented workforce is to adopt a distributed leadership model.

"In the end, it's crucial to build a cohesive team," says Michelle. "You want to be the type of place employees would refer their friends to work."

5

Marketing and Promotional Campaigns

They're More Than Just a Megaphone

5.1 Start at the Beginning

Before creating marketing and promotional campaigns, entrepreneurs need to ask themselves: *what emotions do I want to evoke in my target audiences?* And most importantly, *what specific actions do I want them to take?* Yes, you want the public to buy your product, but drill down deeper. Why should they purchase it multiple times? Why should they refer friends or devote time following you on social media? Your answers are the foundation on which to build a multipronged campaign.

Many entrepreneurs think of promotional campaigns as something to tack on after the launch of their start-up or the rolling out of a new product line. But a more effective approach to developing your story and building your brand is to start well before the launch. Say, during the design phase of your product, one of your answers to your "Why should they buy it?" question is "because I'm going to make my product user friendly." This focus on your customers' needs from your product's inception becomes part of your start-up's story, which you can develop in tandem with your prototype. By thinking about your earliest users' experiences and your company's growth through a promotional lens, you are better positioned to create future marketing campaigns, advertisement copy, tag lines, and social media content. There are many best practices and AI tools to support your promotional efforts at any stage of your start-up's life cycle. A good place to start is best practices around relationship building with reporters.

5.2 The Benefits of Earned Media Coverage

When writing ad copy or promoting yourself through social media, you decide how to define and portray your product and services. "Earned" media coverage, on the other hand, is written by third parties such as journalists and experts. Securing objective third-party coverage in newspapers, magazines, online media outlets, and broadcast programs builds trust and credibility among potential customers and is an excellent way to reach large audiences. Such news coverage is also attractive to investors as well as increasing your rankings on search engines.

We're not going to sugarcoat it. Capturing journalists' attention is challenging, particularly for start-ups. Many reporters at business and broadcast media outlets are cautious about covering start-ups because they're concerned their credibility will be hurt if they fail. You'll thus need to develop news hooks on which to hang your stories. When covering young and growing companies, the following are some topics of interest to reporters:

- Noteworthy awards
- Compelling human interest stories
- Funding announcements
- New partnerships with established organizations
- How your company fits into larger industry or economic trends
- Your company's positive impact on your community

To better understand what resonates with reporters, it's first helpful to spend a morning in their shoes.

Thinking Like a Reporter

Picture starting your day in the newsroom of a prominent daily newspaper where you cover the technology beat in the publication's business bureau. Your co-workers cover the business bureau's additional beats including banking, economics, energy, finance, healthcare, industry news, and manufacturing.

You log onto your computer. Your inbox is stuffed with nearly 100 emails, most of which are pitches from businesses, public relations agencies, and others working in marketing positions. By the end of an average day, you expect roughly 200 emails to find their way into your inbox. With recent cuts to your editorial staff due to declines in advertising dollars, you've lost a junior writer. You are currently on multiple story deadlines.

You skim through your emails and immediately delete those with subject lines about start-up funding news, healthcare innovations, and new company hires. If these entrepreneurs were familiar with your news beat, they'd have known that you only cover technology and would have reached out to the correct journalists who cover these topics.

One subject line that reads "AI start-up reinvents business model" captures your attention. You open the email, which contains a one-line pitch and encourages you to read an attached press release to learn more. For security reasons, you don't open attachments from unknown sources. You delete the email.

Another email you open has a pitch that runs five paragraphs long. You look at the clock—you don't have the bandwidth to figure out if there's a solid news hook, so you delete it.

You open an email with the subject line that reads, "Technology Prototypes on Display at Local Conference"—this is definitely something you'd consider attending. But as you read the pitch, you realize it's a story written about a conference that took place two days ago, which you now consider "old news." Plus, your publication doesn't publish stories written by third parties outside of the newsroom, so you delete it.

You check your phone messages. One start-up has been leaving you repeated messages about their new product. When you're interested in a phone pitch, you typically respond by the first or second call. Can't they take the hint that anything after two calls usually means you're passing? You make a mental note to avoid the start-up's future pitches before deleting the message.

You return to your emails and recognize one from an entrepreneur who regularly follows your social media accounts, likes and shares your posts, and has posted links to your more prominent features on his company website under "Stories Worth Reading," something you really appreciate. He's pitched you a story idea about the growth of his start-up reflecting larger technology trends; while it's not something you can use right now, you move his email to your Ideas folder and ask him to keep you updated on his start-up's growth.

You open another email with a subject line that reads "Smarter than ChatGPT: Start-up's advanced prompt engineering." The pitch, which runs only two paragraphs long, leads with the news hook: a start-up has invented an AI-assisted tool using advanced prompt engineering to generate new ideas to users' questions. For more details, a press release with a link to a video explaining how the AI-assisted tool works, has been pasted underneath the sender's signature.

You pour yourself a cup of coffee and skim the press release. The writing is straightforward, persuasive, and to the point. Now, this may be a story worth pursuing.

Press Material and Pitching Essentials: Best Practices

Here's the thing about press releases: those writing them often forget that their target audience are journalists—the "press" in "press release." By mastering best practices, you are better positioned to write copy that gets picked up.

Avoid "Unique" and "Cutting-Edge" Adjectives

What do the words *unique, cutting-edge, revolutionary, state of the art, leading,* and *groundbreaking* have in common? They're all subjective adjectives. That, and notoriously overused in press material.

Tricia once met with a reporter during the dot-com boom who noted that adjectives like these were so ubiquitous in start-ups' press releases and pitches that he stopped reading the copy whenever he encountered one. More recently, she's spoken with reporters who've made similar observations about the use of these pesky, subjective adjectives in AI press material.

But, you may say, my product offers a completely new way of delivering crucial services—doesn't this make it groundbreaking?

Most likely, yes. But because you and so many other entrepreneurs are using the same descriptors, it's difficult for reporters to discern when your product or service really is unique, cutting-edge, or revolutionary. To appeal to reporters, you need to fall back on a classic literary narrative technique: *show, don't tell.*

Your Press Release's Crucial Opening Paragraph: Don't Bury the Lead   At a media conference Tricia recently attended, one reporter shared that by the second paragraph of a press release or pitch, he knew whether he'd continue reading it. Another reporter on the panel interjected and said that she rarely read past the first paragraph if it didn't grab her interest.

Your opening paragraphs are, in essence, your elevator pitch.

From a very young age, we learn that stories have a beginning and middle that build up to a climatic ending. Think of a press release as an inverse pyramid—you start with the "climatic ending," which may include what specifically your product or service accomplishes and why this is important, the void it fills, or studies supporting your claims. Once established, you can then work backward by focusing on the details your audience needs to know, such as the most effective way to use your product, where the idea came from, and how the founders met, among others.

It's tempting to write a press release or pitch that reads like a commercial. But commercials by their very nature are self-serving, and this approach won't appeal to reporters who aren't in the business of selling your product—they are on the search for stories that will appeal to their target audiences.

Don't Slam the Competition   Your product or service may very well be better than what's currently on the market but slamming the competition paints you in a negative light. By highlighting what you do best or citing studies that back up your improvements or better illustrate the problem, you show journalists your strengths without dragging someone else down.

Repurpose Your Press Release Typically, press releases are distributed over a business wire and received by news offices that subscribe to the wire service. You can boost your visibility beyond journalists with search engine optimization (SEO) by strategically placing keywords in your press release to increase the chances that people searching topics related to your start-up will come across your release. When including the release in a pitch, it's best to paste the copy under your signature so the reporter doesn't need to open an attachment or click on a link.

Most importantly, you now have language to repurpose when pitching reporters and for creating social content, advertisements, tag lines, and other promotional material. And when you start landing interviews, you have a foundation from which to create your key messages.

5.3 Media Training: Make Your Messages Stick

You've secured an interview on a popular morning television program to talk about the positive impact your start-up is making in your community. You recognize it as a golden opportunity to build awareness of your products and services. But as the date of the broadcast creeps up, your tension rises. You want exposure, but standing in the stoplight makes you feel exposed. What if the host tosses an unexpected question at you? What if everyone misinterprets what you say? Even worse, what if you come across as awkward or flub your answer? What if your attempt at raising your profile ends up hurting your business instead?

We spoke with Brad Phillips, founder and CEO of Throughline Group, a media training and public speaking agency. Brad has worked in the field of media training since 2004 following a career as an associate producer for CNN's *Reliable Sources, The Capital Gang*, and *Late Edition with Wolf Blitzer*, as well as a production coordinator for *ABC News Nightline*. His book,

The Media Training Bible,[1] remains one of Amazon's top-selling titles on the topic since its publication in 2012.

Over the years, Brad has media-trained clients from many walks of life including CEOs, company spokespeople, government officials, professors, athletes, and entrepreneurs. When he's asked what prompted their calls, they typically say the same things—they're struggling to get their message across to target audiences or reporters never seem to cover their key points or they're nervous about being judged or they speak too much or too little.

By mastering interview techniques, you are better positioned to promote your company and bolster your reputation by deftly handling whatever questions are thrown at you. In the process, you'll build solid relationships with reporters.

Prepare and Plate an Entrée Versus Taking Reporters to a Buffet Brad often hears this complaint from clients: they've spent a half hour or more interviewing with a reporter only to discover the quotes the reporter selected don't convey any of their key points. A golden opportunity has been wasted.

Brad says this approach to interviewing—and the lackluster results—is much more common than you would think because of:

- The belief that you need to share information about every aspect of your business so reporters have enough background versus focusing on your key messages

- The belief that you need to educate the reporter on topics related to your company or areas of expertise versus speaking to your target audience *through* the reporter

- The belief that you need to passively answer a reporter's every question versus adeptly steering the conversation to your key messages

When it comes to interviewing, Brad uses the analogy of serving reporters a dish that you've prepared and plated with an entrée and a few side dishes versus taking them to a buffet where they'll get to choose from multiple options and fill their plate with food that may not appeal to you.

Crafting Your Three Key Messages and "Message Supports" Brad recommends identifying your three key messages. Why three? "Because this is widely regarded in the media training field as the right balance between too few, which leads to audience boredom—and too many—which leads to low audience retention," he says.

Start by brainstorming, jotting down words and phrases that come top of mind. Then, select the three items you think your target audience wants the most from you. Now you have what you need to flesh out and articulate your top three messages.

Next, Brad recommends creating "message supports." These are:

Stories: A story could be a personal experience, someone else's experience, a case study, or a current or historical event. The point of working a story into an interview is to illustrate and humanize a key message. We are wired to respond to stories—they evoke emotions and create mental images that make your key messages memorable.

Opening quote: *"By investing in infrastructure today, we'll create hundreds of thousands of jobs and resuscitate the manufacturing sector."*

Storytelling quote: *"The owner of one steel factory in Pennsylvania told me that his company is on the verge of bankruptcy but that this bill would keep his factory open and his 200 workers employed."*[2]

Statistics: Raw numbers are often difficult to put into perspective. Your job is to take boring, impersonal numbers and provide them with meaningful context to evoke a strong response.

Statistic: Four-and-a-half million Americans have Alzheimer's disease.

Statistic with impact: *Fenway Park seats 37,000 people. It would take 122 Fenway Parks to hold every American with Alzheimer's disease. That's four-and-a-half million people in total who are afflicted with this awful disease.*[3]

Sound bites: The media loves sound bites, those short and catchy phrases or sentences that sum up a message in a memorable or witty manner. Sound bites often find their way into reporters' quotes to the delight of readers. It's important to note, too, that in the 1960s the average sound bite ran 48 seconds long. Today, the average sound bite is seven seconds. This means distilling your pitch to its very core.

Examples: "The only thing to fear is fear itself" (Franklin D. Roosevelt). "Success is not final, failure is not fatal—it is the courage to continue that counts" (Winston Churchill). "You're gonna need a bigger boat" (Chief Martin Brody, Jaws).

The Interview: Always Stick to Your Key Messages

Brad's advice on how to answer a reporter's questions might surprise you—he recommends tailoring your key messages and message supports in answering every single question. That's right. Every single one.

"I don't mean to repeat your messages verbatim—rather, you need to convey their theme throughout the entire interview and make them memorable, visual, and sticky with the help of your message supports," he says.

While you might think it's okay to go off message at least a couple of times, Brad doesn't advise it. "Let's say the reporter asks you eight questions and you've stayed on message in answering five of them," says Brad. "You may feel good about the interview, but there's now no guarantee the resulting story will contain any of your key messages. Today's wasted answer may be tomorrow's lead quote."

Sometimes the hardest questions are those that are open-ended: "Tell me about your company or your innovation." There's so much to say. This is why key messages are so important for staying on track.

Reporter: Tell me about your toy company.

Typical Answer: Smith Toys is one of the leading companies in the United States making high-quality children's toys in an affordable and sustainable manner.

Memorable Answer: You know how children's toys always seem to cost too much and break within weeks of opening the box? Well, Smith Toys makes toys that are going to work for years after you open the package—we guarantee it—and we've even figured out a way to make high-quality toys that are both affordable and environmentally friendly.[4]

Answering Hard Questions A cyberattack cripples your services. Bad behavior by someone on your leadership team may compromise your brand image. Promised funding falls through. And now, a reporter is on the phone questioning you about it.

"You should answer every question, even the hard ones, every time—if you go with 'no comment,' you risk appearing elusive or even guilty, and the news story will reflect this, to your detriment," says Brad.

To help clients answer difficult questions with ease, Brad has developed a systematic method he calls the ATMs—*Answer, Transition, Message, sell.*

Answer: You can answer off-topic questions in a single word or phrase—"yes," "no," "that's not quite right," "absolutely," or "absolutely not."

Transition: This part is key. Use short answers to build a bridge from the reporter's question to *your* answer. "I can't speak for my COO about his behavior, but what I can say about our company is this . . .," "Here's what we've been hearing from our customers/ donors/investors . . .," "That said, what we see as an even bigger issue is . . .," "Here's what the numbers don't tell you . . .."

Message: Once you've bridged, you can fall back on your key messages to respond.

Sell: Your call to action. You might encourage people to buy your product, visit your website, or support your cause. Brad lowercases the *s* because the sell isn't always appropriate depending on the context.

"The goal of any crisis from a reputational point of view is to keep the news lifecycle as short as possible," stresses Brad. "And this is only possible by handling it properly at the outstart."

One way to calm your nerves? Remember that it's not about you. Brad recommends focusing on your target audience instead of your fears. What do they need from you? What are their concerns? How can you make their lives better? "That, and practice, practice, practice," says Brad. "Interviewing is a skill you can master."

5.4 Leverage AI to Build Your Campaign

We spoke with Gina Carr, COO and co-founder of Stark Raving Entrepreneurs, who helps companies leverage technology, social media, and AI to drive sales and raise business profiles. She is a proponent of using generative AI (GenAI) assistants—which perform tasks based on users' prompts and commands—and agents agentic generative AI (AI agents)—which operate autonomously to achieve the goals users define without the need for user input. Here are best practices she's shared with us:

Dig into your "memory box" for compelling content: Think of your life as your palette and GenAI as your brush to leverage creative content from your "memory box." For instance, if your start-up sells bicycles, share the sense of freedom you experienced as a child pedaling through your neighborhood for the first time. Then convey that joy to potential customers. Depending on your promotional needs, you may want to use prompts to make the copy thoughtful, funny, whimsical, or adventurous. AI can help you add depth and richness to your skeleton of a story. Your goal is to draw people into your world.

Drive potential customers to your lead magnets: Don't just drive traffic to your website—steer them instead to a specific "lead magnet" on a separate landing page. A lead magnet is a free item such as a discount code, coupon, a quiz, an e-publication or guide, a template, or a complementary service—something your target audience finds of value—in exchange for collecting potential customer's contact information, which is typically an email address or cell number. An exit pop-up on your website with a lead magnet offer is another method for enticing people to share their information on the way out the door. If you need ideas, ask your GenAI assistant what would make a good lead magnet for your company. Then, ask the GenAI assistant to help you create and market it.

The intimacy of video: Video content is emotionally digestible and makes people feel like they know you. They see your eyes and hear your voice, which helps build trust over platforms like TikTok and YouTube. By creating a long-form video, you have content to slice and dice into short-form videos to release over a longer period of time.

Strategically choose a central platform: Focus your promotional efforts on a single social media platform versus spreading your content out across multiple platforms. This way you avoid having to learn multiple "languages." So, select the one that will resonate the most with your target audience. If you aren't sure, ask your AI tools for suggestions on which platform will best help you build, engage, and nurture your target audience. On your other social media accounts, create what I call an "out to lunch" note: *Visit me at (name of platform) where I spend most of my time!*

It's all about timing: Organize your promotional campaign into three stages:

Pre-campaign: Planning your campaign, setting goals for specific audiences and target markets, and letting your audience know that something is coming.

Early campaign: Launch in bitesize chunks to your audience. Measure what's working and do more of it (and less of what isn't).

Post campaign: Measure the results and identify core wins and losses. Rinse and repeat. Add urgency, scarcity, and social proof to your offers.

Time parameters: Ask your AI tools to make recommendations about the time parameters of a campaign—when it's best to launch, the proposed duration of the campaign, your goals of launching it, and your desired outcome.

Building relationships takes time: Just as in real life, building great social media relationships takes time and effort. This means showing up now and then with "flowers" (your lead magnets) and staying in touch through email and texts. It may take you anywhere from three to six months to connect. But remember, you're in this relationship for the long haul!

As Gina points out, video content is emotionally digestible. Audiences see your eyes, hear your voice, and connect with your personality. Next we'll meet an unlikely entrepreneur who leveraged YouTube to become one of Italy's online sensations.

Errico Porzio, who innovated on pizza in the city where it was born.
Photo credit: Courtesy of Errico Porzio.

5.5 Errico Porzio's "Social Pizza"

How do you innovate on pizza in the Italian city where it was first created?[5] For Errico Porzio, it meant launching what he calls *social pizza*.

Born into an impoverished area of Naples, Italy, Errico's relationship with pizza making began at the age of 14 when an entrepreneurial uncle, who worked long and hard to buy a pizzeria, offered him a job. Driven to improve his circumstances, it wasn't uncommon for Errico to work 16-hour shifts helping to produce anywhere from 300 to 400 pizzas a day. He later went on to work in some of Naples' finest restaurants.

Errico founded and self-funded his first pizzeria in 2012. As his venture grew, he identified three elements to differentiate himself in a city crowded with pizzerias: product creativity, top-notch culinary skills, and creating a social media presence.

Errico calls his creative process "l'arte bianca" or "white art." When he contemplates the soft dough moving through his hands, he's at his creative best. L'arte bianca helped him put his own spin on pizza a portafoglio (wallet pizza), a traditional Neapolitan street food made by folding a pizza into quarters so that it resembles a wallet.[6] This portable dish is ideal for people on the go who hold the crust with the point of the slice tucked inside the folds and eat it from the outside in without losing the toppings. Errico's wallet pizzas took social media—in particular, TikTok and Instagram—by storm, creating buzz among Italians and a surge in sales that allowed him to grow his business.

"Authenticity is crucial in building rapport with Errico's three million social media followers," says Luca Morieri, Errico's social media manager. "Errico brings energy and a relaxed vibe into the kitchen where followers are privy to his creative process. Errico engages with followers by sharing how to replicate his favorite dishes at home and responding to their requests for how-to culinary videos of a recipe they're eager to learn. We also concentrate on themes and holidays. For instance, last Valentine's Day we created a video about food and romance, which was well-received."

Luca posts spontaneous moments and interactions throughout the pizza maker's day. This communications strategy shifted into high gear during the COVID lockdown, allowing Errico to seamlessly enter viewers' homes with a focus on comfort food, which in turn spiked take-out orders. While other restaurants closed, Errico's chain thrived and expanded.

"By alternating between the Neapolitan dialect and the Italian language, Errico endeared himself through his videos to his local, core customer base and leveraged that popularity to become an

Italian phenomenon," said Francesco Schiavone, a professor in management at the University of Naples – Parthenope.

While Errico brings together ingredients that look visually stunning, he's well aware that you need substance behind an image if you want to succeed in the long run.

"I only use local, seasonal ingredients," says Errico. "For example, spring and summer mean lighter pizzas with a focus on vegetables like zucchini, eggplant, and arugula. The menus may differ depending on what's grown in the various regions where my pizzerias are located. I don't use any mass-produced products and have built exclusive relationships with suppliers who offer high-quality products and ingredients. And speaking of ingredients, I never use more than four in a dish to avoid sensory overload. I integrate ingredients in novel ways, forms, and textures such as chopping, slicing, or dicing them into shapes that work together or turn a vegetable like zucchini into an exquisite cream sauce."

Errico founded and self-funded Pizzeria Errico Porzio in 2012 and now has 10 restaurants in the Campania region of Italy. In 2018, he expanded his business in several ways: he adopted a to-go franchise model and opened 10 storefronts that sell pizza slices and food to go, extended his brand with two specialty food stores called Ciao Mamma, and launched a pizza making school. The school has been particularly appealing to tourists who are a focus of the school's marketing campaign and offers Errico a way to train employees to work at his pizzerias.

Sales in 2024 were approximately $20 million and are expected to rise with the introduction of these new revenue streams. Errico boasts the largest chain in Italy directly controlled by the owner.

Italians aren't typically fond of pineapple pizza, so Errico pokes fun at it by slicing mozzarella in a way that resembles a pineapple. And he's invested in new Google glasses integrated with a camera for recording videos that allow for a deeper dive into the ingredients and methods he uses in his creative process.

Whether it's social media or marketing material, Errico encourages entrepreneurs to "be yourself. If you aren't authentic, people will see through you."

5.6 Digital Marketing Best Practices

According to Jake Cook, understanding how your ideal customer thinks about and searches for products and services similar to yours will generate insights that will translate into sales. Jake is the CEO of the digital marketing firm Tadpull and a lecturer in the marketing unit at HBS where he teaches a course on digital marketing and AI. His research focuses on how companies design and scale customer acquisition and retention strategies using digital marketing, data, and performance-driven decision-making with AI. Jake sat down with us to share his insights:

SEO—You're Known By the Company You Keep With your ideal customer profile in mind, experiment with search word combinations that describe your product or service to see how they're ranked by top online search engines. Each search engine uses its own algorithms to calculate and rank search terms. Investing in a few digital advertisements is a good way to determine how your word combinations rank and how they're being used. Think of the money spent on digital ads as less of an operating expense and more of a discovery process for a higher return on future advertising. Creating interview scripts and incentives to survey potential customers on how they search can guide you through this process as well.

Free tools such as Google Trends analyze search words and phrases on Google Search. Over time, you can create a graph showing how often your search terms are used and in what locations. You can then use the data for search engine optimization (SEO) and advertising and content creation.

You can also use these methods to analyze your competition. Jake recommends focusing on five top competitors—review their comments, ratings, and rankings and put them all into ChatGPT to analyze and build intelligence around patterns.

Rising to the Top in Organic Searches   There's paid online searches and advertisements to bolster your ranking, and then there's appearing near or at the top of organic online searches in your category. Identifying the highest ranked search terms for your product is the first step.

For example, Jake once worked with a start-up bringing to market a ruggedized backpack for military use. The founders experimented with word combinations they *assumed* would appeal to prospective customers. They tried "ruggedized backpacks," "military backpacks," and "hardened backpacks." Through experimentation, they finally hit on the right word combination— "military assault backpacks"—that ranked at the top of search terms for backpacks similar to theirs.

Now, the company was positioned to create content—such as case studies, earned media coverage, videos, expert commentary, and opinion pieces—that would include the search term *military assault backpacks* with the goal of achieving a high rank in organic searchers. Search engines, in turn, will recognize the volume of content as evidence that you know your market really well, which will improve your organic search rankings. However, if you flood a search engine with press releases that merely claim your expertise in a given area, the search engines will recognize this and will not credit your search ranking. It'll take time to ascend the ranks of the top organic search terms you desire, but it's well worth the effort to generate a stream of quality content in which you serve as the expert in your market.

Create an Email List, but Avoid Spamming   With so much focus on AI, it's easy to overlook email marketing campaigns. Most founders assume they can simply buy a list of prospects and market to them. But there's no guarantee that the list is up-to-date or of good quality. Instead, build your own email and text number lists of people who express interest in your product.

This is a key learning—you cannot outsource the knowledge of your potential customers. Treat your list with great care, and avoid spamming them with every single offer. Instead, market thoughtful content to these lists and keep them informed of news about your company that could be useful to them. And don't let AI write your emails. You can use AI to generate ideas, but you want to retain a human touch.

Referral Traffic: Be Aware of "Walled-in Gardens"   You can post teasers on websites like LinkedIn or Reddit with wording like, "To read more, visit my site," followed by posting your link. Google keeps track of which websites refer traffic to your site so you can track how it impacts your organic ranking. But it's a complex relationship—these sites are both partners for and competitors of your traffic. Typically, after someone clicks your link, a message will pop up asking, "Are you sure you want to leave this site?" In effect, they are creating what Jake calls a "walled-in garden" that may or may not influence potential customers to visit your website.

It's a Journey, Not a Destination   Just because you make a sale doesn't mean you can make it scale. If you're committed to increasing your revenue and operational capacity without proportional increases in costs, you need to stay on top of ever-evolving AI technology. Constantly be testing, iterating, searching, and learning how to use new AI tools. If you think of digital marketing as a journey versus a destination, you will better position yourself to rank at the top.

Next, we'll meet an unlikely entrepreneur who's taken out-of-the-box thinking to a whole new level in marketing campaigns that even captured the attention of the business world's unofficial marketing and advertising bible.

5.7 Scott Ginsberg: Titan Casket, Funeral Industry Disrupter: Marketing Mortality by Thinking Outside the Box

It's expensive to die in the United States. According to the National Funeral Directors Association, the median cost of a funeral with a viewing and burial comes in around $8,000.[7] Mind you, this doesn't include the cost of a burial plot, vault, headstone, flowers, obituary, reception, or the small, personal touches that memorialize the passing of a loved one.

A casket is often the single most expensive purchase[8] in a traditional funeral service due in part to a "duopoly": there are two casket providers—the Batesville Casket Company and

Matthews Aurora Funeral Solutions—that sell directly to funeral homes and account for more than 80% of all casket sales in the country.[9] As a result, they play an outsized role in setting prices that reverberate throughout the entire industry.

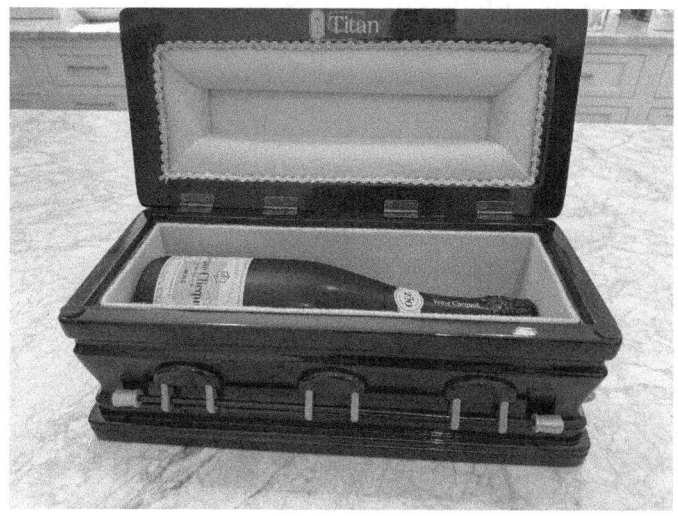

The Titan Casket Wine Holder is perfect for storing your favorite beverage.

Photo credit: Scott Ginsberg.

Depressing? Not if you're an entrepreneur who recognizes a $20 billion casket industry ripe for innovation.

Titan Casket, the company Scott co-founded in 2016, has since grown into the largest online, direct-to-consumer seller of caskets and funeral products in the United States offering consumers a selection of more than 1,000 casket models and urns. In 2025, the company grossed approximately $8 million.

A driver of Titan's impressive performance has been its unconventional approach to marketing mortality in thoughtful and humorous ways. *Ad Age*—the business world's unofficial bible for insights and analysis on advertising, marketing, and media—named

Titan Casket as one of only 10 Marketers to Watch in 2025[10] in their brand category "following a year of innovative and edgy marketing campaigns that have garnered attention and solidified Titan Casket's position as a disruptive force in the funeral industry."

Not bad for a guy who was once described as a "ship without a rudder."

Galloping down an entrepreneurial path was once the farthest thing from Scott's mind. But he possesses two qualities that helped propel him to success: Scott has a very different relationship with failure than most people do. That, and a sense of curiosity so acute it has negated self-doubts and insecurities, leading him to explore educational and career paths off the beaten trail.

I Can Do That Scott grew up on Massachusetts' North Shore in a household that valued hard work and securing a stable job just as Scott's father, Larry Ginsberg, had done through a career in real estate. Larry took pride in providing for his family, reflecting the values he brought from his hardscrabble upbringing in a working-class city outside of Boston. But when applying to colleges became a hot topic among Scott's peer group, he didn't want to be left out although he wasn't sure where to start.

"Take the SATs," his friends told him with a warning that the test was hard. Scott sized up his friends' brainpower and thought, *I can do that*. Little did he know that these four words would become his mantra, taking him down unusual and unexpected paths.

To his surprise, Scott performed well on the test. Following graduation, Scott shouldered various jobs while attending night classes at Salem State University with a few courses at Boston University sprinkled in. If you asked Scott if he had a career in mind, he would answer vaguely about working for a business someday. What type of business he didn't know.

Around this time, Scott dated a woman he'd met at Boston University whose father had taken an interest in Scott's career path or, rather, lack of one. He noted that while Scott showed a lot of potential, he was like a ship without a rudder. Scott recalls, "He told me I needed to embrace education as a lifelong endeavor in whatever form it took, because even though someone or something could take away all my money, no one could take away my education. That really stuck with me, giving me a renewed sense of purpose."

He was going to need it.

Culture Shock   The spark in Scott and his girlfriend's relationship quickly cooled to a small ember. Since they still cared for one another, he made a bold suggestion—they should set each other up on blind dates. This is how Scott met Stephanie, the woman he'd one day marry. In an interesting twist, his girlfriend married the guy Scott set her up with.

Over an evening meal with Stephanie and her family months into their relationship, her sister shared exciting news: she'd been accepted into an eight-week summer language immersion program offered by Middlebury College located in a bucolic Vermont town where she would study Chinese.

"I thought the concept of an immersion language program sounded so cool," says Scott. "What was stopping me from enrolling, too?" With his I-can-do-that attitude—and most of his savings—he was accepted into the college's Spanish immersion program, much to the dismay of his family.

While Scott had anticipated being exposed to a new culture, he hadn't anticipated a culture shock of a different kind. From the way his new peers dressed to their life experiences and goals to their cultural references, there were class differences. But with curiosity steering the wheel, Scott fit in. One new friendship in particular would inspire him in an unexpected way.

"A guy who lived across from my dorm room told me he'd been accepted into Columbia Business School. I liked him and all, but he was no genius. I reasoned that if he could get into a top-ranked Ivy League school, why couldn't I?"

While Scott was a smart guy, his grades didn't reflect this. His courses at Salem State hadn't ignited any sparks, and he was just going through the motions and earning Bs and Cs. So he chose to share his GMAT scores with Columbia Business School (CBS) instead because . . . why not?

Scott was authentically himself during his in-person interview. "I was working at a lending company at the time and dealing with foreclosures, so I shared how I repossessed a hearse with the body still in it. This caught the admissions officer's attention."

And it worked. In 1993, Scott was accepted into CBS's Master of Business Administration (MBA) program without yet having completed his undergraduate degree. "Business schools today tend to look for form over substance," he says. "If this was the case back then, there's no way I would have even landed the interview."

When Scott received the Ivy league business school's acceptance letter, his parents were perplexed. "They asked me if I planned on becoming a professor." When pressed about his career path, he admitted he didn't really have one. "My goal was exposure," he says. "I was on a journey to meet and learn from people smarter than me."

Flash-forward a few months into Scott's business school journey. He was struggling with a steep workload and had taken on serious debt. If he failed, there was no security net to break his fall. Sure, he'd walk away with gained business knowledge, but without an MBA from or a network built at Columbia he'd most likely drown in debt and hear "I told you so" from family. He credits his love of high school gymnastics as a source of his academic success.

"The way I look at it, I practiced in the gym every single day and failed every single day in the process. And every single failure took me closer to mastering new skills. Instead of fearing failure, I leaned in and had fun with it."

Scott graduated from CBS in 1995, and while he wasn't close to the top of his class, he quickly secured a position at Orbitex Group Funds selling financial services throughout Latin America. His investment in Middlebury's Spanish immersion program paid itself off.

Soon, in the most unexpected way, Scott would find himself honing a skill set for a role he'd never envisioned taking on—that of entrepreneur.

Laying Titan Casket's Foundation   The road to Titan Casket began with a failed loan. Scott's father Larry, who was making loans as a side business, found himself the owner of a warehouse packed with 200 caskets after the company went into foreclosure. Scott built a website and database for his father's new business, initially focusing on selling caskets directly to consumers.

Key to this venture was the "Funeral Rule" established in 1984 by the Federal Trade Commission[11] to ensure consumers have the right to provide a casket by their own means, which meant Scott could legally ship a casket or other funeral products purchased online to any funeral home or residence across the United States. He also targeted funeral homes to tap into the most effective distribution network available at that time.

Shortly after, a family friend approached Scott with an opportunity to work on the outsourcing side of manufacturing caskets. He jumped at the chance. After a few years of gaining vital experience, Scott felt confident enough to launch his first start-up, Northern Craft Casket, which manufactured and sold customized, high-quality caskets to funeral homes.

For the welding and grinding involved in the caskets' creation, Scott hired vocational students. He then turned his focus to sales and overseeing a staff of nearly 40 employees and brought on a relative on board to oversee production, which turned out to be a mistake. "The handles on our first order of caskets all fell off."

Scott discovered how difficult it feels to lay off a family member and, later, other employees. "It's one of the hardest parts about running a company," he says. "But it's the reality of being a business owner—you have to be willing to pivot." And pivot he did. Scott chose to outsource the manufacturing of the caskets to focus on expanding sales throughout the Northeast. But then he smacked up against his family's reputation. "The region's tight-knit funeral industry frowned on my father selling directly to consumers, even though I knew other funeral homes were selling within their own families," he says.

Scott experienced firsthand what he describes as the lumbering pace of innovation in the U.S. multibillion-dollar funeral industry populated with an estimated 20,000 funeral homes,[12] many of which, he says, were led by directors who weren't businesspeople: funeral homes were often inherited, and families tended to hold on tightly to tradition and a business model resistant to change.

Two large accounts folded after they learned of Scott's ties to his father, resulting in more than $1 million of lost revenue. Fortunately for Scott, he was about to fail spectacularly in pivoting where he would need it most—on a New England mountainside's black diamond ski slope.

The *Aha!* Moment One week earlier, Scott's family had implored him to join them for a last run down a challenging ski slope nestled in the White Mountains of New Hampshire. Scott was tired but relented. He adjusted his hat, which covered a headset, so he could continue making work calls. Halfway down, the lead edge of his ski caught in the snow and resisted turning in its desired direction. Scott heard a sickening popping sound—he'd blown out his knee's ACL.

Now, Scott's injured leg was clamped into a machine that bent it back and forth for hours at a time. The monotony was stifling. So, he decided to list a casket on Amazon to gauge how well it would be received. To his surprise, it sold. He posted another. That one sold, too. Before long, sales began to roll in.

Scott realized he was onto something—why not launch a start-up that sold caskets only online? By purchasing from contract manufacturers, he could sell directly to the public at reduced prices. An online business would also greatly increase the number of caskets and funeral products people could view from the comforts of home.

Scott chose the name Titan for his start-up. The largest moon of Saturn, Titan embodied strength, scale, and resilience—qualities he wanted the brand to represent. Plus he enjoyed comic books, and Titan had a presence in the Marvel and DC Universe.

Scott set out to identify a vendor manager to help guide him through the process of selling at scale on Amazon. With a little research, he identified around one dozen CBS alumni employed in various roles. One new connection Scott cold called—and future Titan co-founder—was Josh Siegal, a Columbia MBA who'd graduated 13 years after Scott and led shipment of Amazon's large-item retail categories, experience that would greatly benefit Titan.

Josh was intrigued by Scott's proposed business model. Over dinner, the duo reflected on Warby Parker, which had revolutionized the eyewear industry by offering direct-to-consumer options. They asked themselves, why couldn't Titan Casket become the "Warby Parker" of caskets?

Titan Casket launched in 2016 with Scott assuming the role of CEO and co-founders Josh serving as chief operating officer and his talented wife Liz Siegal assuming the role of chief customer officer.

The Titan team chose central locations for five warehouses across the country to serve the most people in different segments of the country while ensuring enough overlap if severe weather impacts one of its locations. They targeted those actively searching for caskets by investing in Google keywords; search engine optimization remains one of Titan Casket's most important marketing tools. But the leadership team didn't want Titan Casket to morph into a faceless supplier. After all, these were people mourning the loss of loved ones. When they launched their website in 2020, they introduced a Talk to a Trusted Expert button, which allows for an instant online chat. Callers are greeted by a sales team sensitive to their loss.

"Our focus isn't on pushing products; it's about answering questions, educating callers on cost, offering suggestions on what works for their budget, and how best to honor a loved one with personal or customized touches," says Scott. Thanks to this empathetic approach, nearly three-fourths of their sales take place on Titan Casket's website.

Now, the Titan team felt ready to take their marketing strategy to a whole new level.

Taylor Swift: End of an Eras   The phone call came through to Titan Casket from a Hollywood production house requesting to buy a customized casket for a music video. Titan's team had no idea how the casket would be used, but they hoped the video would feature a prominent singer. Their wish would be granted and then some.

In the fall of 2022, pop legend Taylor Swift peeked out of one of their Orion copper caskets with a sunburst pattern on its interior fabric in the music video for her hit song *Anti-Hero*.[13] She even posted the casket on her Instagram and Twitter accounts.

Titan immediately wrote a press release and distributed it over the business wire and their social media accounts. Media coverage and interview requests followed with Titan appearing in publications like *Business Insider*, *Fast Company*, and *Bloomberg*, among others.

An Absurd Request   Scott followed Marques Brownlee (aka MKBHD), a YouTube influencer with approximately 20.1 million followers[14] best known for his videos reviewing technology devices. Scott composed an email to Marques with a subject line that read, "Absurd Request: Review a Casket." How could you not open an email like that? Marques' interest was also piqued by Titan's Taylor Swift connection. So, Scott found out Marques' favorite color, rented a U-Haul moving truck, loaded a bright red metal casket with a white satin interior, and drove it to New Jersey. In March 2023, Marques opened an episode by popping out of the casket,[15] which he reviewed, and spoke about Titan's mission to make purchasing a casket more affordable as a clip from Swift's music video flashed across the screen.

Afterward, Marques asked Scott what he was supposed to do with the casket. Scott suggested tossing technology that Marques felt needed to be retired into the casket after conducting a comical burial ceremony. Marques ran with the idea in an episode in November 2022.

Scott refers to his "Absurd Request" email as a Hail Mary pass, a move he's comfortable executing because "it never hurts to ask," he says.

Grave Conversations   One scene in particular in Swift's *Anti-Hero* video stood out for Scott. As she peeks out of the casket and watches her make-believe family fight over her possessions, Swift inadvertently flagged a topic near and dear to his heart—that of normalizing conversations about death and end-of-life planning to achieve peace of mind.

This sentiment was shared by Elan Gale, a television actor, writer, and producer who created the reality series *FBOY Island* after working on *The Bachelor* franchise. Scott and Elan met through a company that financed Titan Casket, and Elan joined the company as their creative director in 2023. "Elan is a creative force who constantly pushes us beyond our comfort zone and challenges us to think in entirely new ways—truly outside the box, no pun intended," says Scott. "Our team holds brainstorming sessions where we throw out crazy ideas to see what sticks."

In 2024, Titan created *Grave Conversations*,[16] a series that has stacked up more than 10 million views on social media platforms hosted by Elan's friend David Dastmalchian whose movie credits include *Dune*, *The Dark Knight*, *The Suicide Squad*, and *Oppenheimer*. The program features Dastmalchian and a celebrity guest lying prone in a Titan casket of their choice pondering universal questions around life and death. Celebrity guests have included, among others, Kumail Nanjiani (*Silicon Valley*, *The Big Sick*), Jack Quaid (*The Hunger Games*), and Kate Siegel (Netflix's *The Fall of the House of Usher*). While the discussion may sound heavy, the mood and dialogue are surprisingly lighthearted with the goal of elevating death from its perception of being a taboo topic. Shot primarily from above, the set includes a table placed between the two caskets set with tea, an urn, flowers, and Titan-branded mugs.

"It's the one thing we can all 100% guarantee is going to happen to each of us at some point, and it's going to happen to every person we love. And it's sad," Dastmalchian said in a March 2024 edition of the *Hollywood Reporter*,[17] adding of that saying goodbye and honoring those we lose: "There's also so much joy and beauty in that process." Dastmalchian also serves as Titan Casket's "ambassador celebrity," appearing in their marketing material.

Meet Mort, Titan's Casket's fuzzy
mascot.

Photo Credit: Scott Ginsberg.

Thinking Outside of the Box   More creative, out-of-the-box
brainstorming with Elan, combined with another of Scott's Hail
Mary passes, led to a collaboration with movie star Ryan
Reynolds' production company Maximum Effort to create a viral
video starring Dastmalchian's commercial on "burying" daylight
saving time.[18] Other brainstorming sessions led to the creation of
the Hydro-Casket, a 12-gauge stainless steel casket model resembling Tesla's Cybertruck that they promoted as the "fastest casket
to heaven." It even comes with a seatbelt.

Brainstorming sessions led to the creation of Titan's mascot Mort (short for mortality, of course), a casket with a friendly
face and little arms and legs. Mort is sold as a plushie through
their online store that also features a mini-casket wine holder
made of cherry wood with a cream-colored interior ideal for

storing a wine bottle. In the summer of 2025, Scott, dressed in a Mort costume, playfully entertained crowds at a Worcester Red Sox game in central Massachusetts as part of Titan's team sponsorship and ran across the field in a race with other corporate mascots.

Putting a creative spin on popular advertisements launched on social media has further supported Titan's marketing efforts. For example, Dunkin Donut's "America Runs on Dunkin" has been reimagined as "America Rests in Titan Casket" with pictures of small caskets replacing the donuts that appear in the advertisement's small boxes.

It's no wonder Titan Casket joined the likes of global, multibillion-dollar companies Calvin Klein, Ferrari, and IMAX as one of only 10 Marketers to Watch in 2025[19] in *Ad Age*'s brand category.

Growing by Leaps and Bounds   Scott had first reached out to Walmart nearly two decades earlier while working with his father to pitch the concept of selling caskets directly to consumers. Great idea, wrong time. Now, multinational and members-only retail corporations have been receptive to working with Titan Casket in newly created online funeral categories. Sam's Club became Titan Casket's first corporate supplier followed by Walmart. Later that year, Titan Casket launched a virtual military line with Costco, which had first experimented with in-store casket sales back in 2005. In 2021, airfreight as a delivery option opened up sales to new locations and saw Titan Casket's first delivery to Hawaii. By the end of the year the company had grown by 400%. Titan has since introduced eco-friendly caskets for green funerals and a pet line of caskets for beloved cats and dogs.

The company has complemented their merchandising with the introduction of a pre-plan service. Now, people can take the prudent step of locking in the cost of a casket and drawing up a contract to have it delivered once there is a need. Titan Casket also wrapped up a series A round of funding, raising $3.5 million in the seed round led by Reformation Partners.

"Jumping into the unknown and the fear of failure can hold you back, so you must grow comfortable with exceeding your grasp," says Scott. "Make it a habit and learn how to be comfortable when things don't work out. Even after you've established a successful venture, every time you hit a milestone there's another path you'll need to explore to keep growing and staying relevant. How do you recognize what should come next? By staying curious."

CHAPTER

6

Reframing Failure
The Art of the Pivot

6.1 The Silence of Failure

The numbers are stark: 10% of start-ups fail within the first year, 70% fail within two to five years, and up to 90% may fail overall. Failure rates are similar across all industries.[1]

If you've read this far, you understand the reasons why the percentage of start-ups that go under is so high and, through our and our experts' advice, how to better position yourself to avoid this fate. In particular, the problem with the "problem" is embedded in too many untested ideas, leading to the failure of companies that never should have become companies in the first place.

Inevitably, at various stages of your entrepreneurial journey, challenges will present themselves. There's the possibility, too, of "black swan" events—a terrorist or cyberattack, a natural disaster, pandemic, or unexpected market turmoil that may wreak havoc with the most well-thought-out plans.

Staring down any type of failure, regardless of its cause, is disheartening and often embarrassing. It's even harder to talk about it. Failure most often brings silence. As a result, some entrepreneurs go to great lengths to cover up their bad luck, mistakes, or lack of knowledge. But this leads to overlooking the real value of failure—if you learn from it, failure becomes your superpower. If you don't, you're bound to repeat your mistakes over and over in different ways and in different settings.

Avoid Creating a Culture of Optics

Have you ever peered into a circus mirror? The curved glass distorts how you really look, creating an optical illusion. Companies that embrace a culture of distorted optics stare into their personal circus mirror and try to convince themselves that what they see is real. And when they try to portray underwhelming results as better than they really are, they signal to everyone in the company to follow suit. This creates a corrosive culture.

As the founder, you have the most up-to-date metrics about your business. It's up to you to interpret and communicate this data honestly. Likewise, it's on you to ground your company culture in honesty and to frame failure for what it really is: a logical evolution in a fast-growing company. It's not something to deny. If you handle failure with care, you relegate it to the ups and downs of your company's journey.

The first step in turning failure around is to understand your role in it. Take a good look in the mirror—not a circus mirror but a real mirror—and be honest with yourself. What room for improvement in your knowledge or behavior has this challenging event revealed? Being truthful with yourself and owning your shortcomings is humbling—it's easier to revel in victimhood and blame someone or something else for your failure versus understanding how, even if inadvertently, you contributed to it. Sometimes it helps when a professional steps in.

The Importance of Being Coachable

Will Keller is the founder and CEO of InterActive Global Coaching. He coaches mid-career professionals and corporate teams at key junctures to build their self-awareness and strengthen leadership skills.

"I'm typically called in when a business is failing," says Will, an entrepreneur who once served as general manager and senior vice president of the Home Shopping Network (HSN). In Will's experience, many founders become so consumed with building their company, they lose perspective and enter into "survival mode," compromising their capacity to acknowledge what is and isn't working.

"Founders often fail to recognize that they need 'shock absorbers' to manage the many bumps in the road they will face," he says. "Without them, every bump seems like the valley of death."

Exacerbating the situation are the long hours entrepreneurs typically work, further draining their reserves. "Heightened emotions will end up controlling you. Founders need to develop a sense of what I call the 'right level of caring.'"

To get the most out of coaching, Will stresses that one needs to *want* to be coached. Otherwise, it may create a "boss versus the coach" dynamic. "I end up hearing from clients like these that they're the ones doing things the right way—it's everyone else who isn't. The world doesn't work that way," says Will.

Will says to be open to coaching is to be open to new concepts, practices, and ways of thinking about your work. "It's learning cues to know which emotions to deploy. I'll say, 'Tell me about a win and a loss'. I make clients realize they're going in the right direction. It's not about what you should stop doing but what actions you can choose to take instead."

Will also role-plays a client's competition. "It's an effective way to examine what your competition is doing right and what type of actions you may want to adopt to do even better."

Most importantly, being "coachable" takes practice. "The only way to make new behaviors stick is repetition," says Will. "That, and the desire to change."

6.2 The Art of the Pivot: Saving Your Company by Killing the Idea You Love

Many, if not all, start-ups pivot at some point. Pivoting involves adjusting or changing the product and/or business model over the span of its existence. Entrepreneurs who are open to pivoting stand a much higher chance of achieving success versus those who refuse to pivot. Why is this?

Optimism is synonymous with entrepreneurship. It's what propels founders forward and convinces them that their idea is desperately needed. In essence, they fall in love with their idea. Because of this infatuation, entrepreneurs run the risk of not listening to market signals or investors who, recognizing lackluster sales, remain unconvinced. Ironically, this pushback from key stakeholders may result in the founder doubling down and falling deeper in love with their idea.

No one wants to hear that their "baby" isn't beautiful. The fact that sales aren't materializing could mean there simply isn't a strong enough need for your idea or perhaps the market isn't ready yet. But some entrepreneurs become convinced they're touching the future and that society and all its potential customers will eventually adapt to the entrepreneur's way of thinking—the market just doesn't understand this yet.

Such a mindset often results in low sales or the need for more financing and may even lead to the founder being removed from the company by investors who want to see if a change in strategy will save their investment. If the entrepreneur isn't willing to pivot, the investors will.

Some pivots are very subtle such as modifying pricing, repositioning the product, or rebranding. Then there are major pivots like the one that pulled a start-up called Spoiler Alert out of its death spiral.

6.3 Ricky Ashenfelter and Emily Malina, Spoiler Alert: Saving Excess Inventory from Landfills

Emily Malina and Ricky Ashenfelter are the co-founders of Spoiler Alert, a start-up that operates at the intersection of waste prevention and business-to-business commerce. Spoiler Alert offers a technological solution for companies grappling with excess and aging inventory, among them fresh and preserved food, personal care items, and other fast-moving consumer goods. By connecting brands with a network of retailers and wholesalers looking for discounted inventory, Spoiler Alert ensures these products reach consumers rather than costly corporate write-offs destined for landfills.

Spoiler Alert launched in 2015 with a different business model, one that initially showed great promise. But it took a

Ricky Ashenfelter and Emily Malina, co-founders of SpoilerAlert.
Photo credit: Liz Linder.

smartly executed pivot by its founders to rescue it from a near-death experience and transform it into the thriving company it is today.

Early Success: A False Perception of a Market Fit   For more than two years, the duo worked one floor apart at Deloitte Consulting where Ricky oversaw energy and supply chain analyses for Fortune 500 food, retail, and consumer packaged goods (CPG) companies, and Emily led complex technology implementations within the federal government. Their paths finally crossed in 2013 at an event on the MIT Sloan campus where they'd both arrived as newly enrolled MBA students. They quickly connected over shared interests and a common concern: the country's massive amount of food waste. According to Feeding America, 145 billion meals' worth of food ends up in U.S. landfills every year.[2]

MIT's rich entrepreneurial ecosystem convinced them to step away from furthering their consulting careers. They eventually developed an app for companies to donate their surplus food items at risk of going to waste by connecting them with organizations interested in attaining them.

Emily and Ricky recruited Massachusetts-based food organizations, which included retailers, manufacturers, distributors, and food-recovery nonprofits, to take part in a pilot program. Over the course of two months, the app helped the organizations to connect at various points of the supply chain. Approximately 8,000 pounds of food had been posted for donation, and Ricky and Emily felt confident about Spoiler Alert's future. The cofounders made the app free to organizations interested in donating food and introduced a subscription-based model for other users.

In rapid succession, Spoiler Alert secured a $50,000 grant after winning the prestigious 2015 MassChallenge competition,[3] a $100,000 grant from the Rockefeller Foundation,[4] and nearly $400,000 in pre-seed funding through Techstars.[5] Ricky also secured a spot on *Forbes* magazine's 30 Under 30 list.[6] These wins culminated with the signing of Sysco, one of the world's largest broadline food service distributors, as their first paying customer,[7] which ultimately allowed the team to close a proper $2.5 seed round from Acre Venture Partners, Valley Oak Investments, and the Betsy and Jesse Fink Family Foundation. More positive press coverage and high-profile endorsements followed when it seemed all but certain that success was in the wings. Spoiler Alert was on a roll.

Or so they thought. One year after closing their first big order and building a sales and marketing team, they were unable to land another ideal customer like Sysco. There were prospects interested in talking to Spoiler Alert about food waste issues and solutions, but few were willing to pay for Spoiler Alert's software product, which they perceived as addressing a discretionary, philanthropic matter (i.e., donations) rather than one rooted in profit and loss impact.

"Our initial success created a false perception of a product market fit," says Ricky. "We took too long to acknowledge that there wasn't a burning desire among our potential customers to activate their budget for Spoiler Alert. It was then that we realized we were tackling the right problem from the wrong angle."

When founders rack up early successes, it becomes harder to recognize when a business model may not have staying power. By 2019, Ricky and Emily were running short of capital and were forced to make a hard decision—should they double down on their original vision and continue searching for more customers similar to Sysco? Or should they pivot? The co-founders decided on the latter.

Assuming they'd be unable to raise additional funding without more defensible traction, they reduced their expenses, cutting their staff by 30%, a painful but necessary decision. This is known as "reducing your cash burn rate," which extends the life of the company. Next, Ricky and Emily re-examined their value proposition and discovered that with major adjustments to their business model they could unlock a segment of customers who would be willing to pay for a waste prevention software platform. This marked a significant shift in their product offering on the supply and demand sides of their marketplace, core value proposition, economic buyers, and their pricing model.

"We looked at our customer pain points differently the second time around," says Ricky. "Our initial focus was on corporations interested in making an impact through charitable donations of food that would go to waste. But this didn't drive revenue or increase efficiency, nor were these efforts managed by teams that had access to discretionary budgets. Now, by shifting our focus to the creation of a platform that helps large CPG companies better understand their inventory issues while offering them support in selling extra inventory for the largest value as possible, we're helping them reduce their write-offs and driving incremental sales while still keeping food and products out of landfills."

The results of this pivot were truly remarkable. Spoiler Alert's sales grew from $100,000 in 2019 when they executed the pivot to nearly $8 million five years later supported along the way by an $11M Series A led by Collaborative Fund.

Had Emily and Ricky stubbornly stuck to their original value proposition they would have gone out of business. Instead, they had the courage to reduce their expenses, re-examine their value proposition, redesign their product, and approach new customers.

"To date, our customers have kept more than 1.7 billion pounds of product out of landfills," says Emily. "This positively impacts corporate profits, the environment and millions of Americans looking to save money."

6.4 The Murder Board: Killing an Idea or Strengthening It

Just as pivoting your company can save you from failure, so can analyzing a problem to death.

Twenty-five years of service in the military including multiple tours in Iraq and Afghanistan has provided retired US Army Colonel Hise O. Gibson with extensive insights into the intricacies of operations and strategic management, lessons he now shares with students at HBS.

Experience has taught Hise the value of critically examining and questioning every aspect of an idea/plan/proposal. While in the army he was an advocate of the "murder board" approach, which, to civilian ears, sounds like a game of *Clue* gone off the rails. The term, which originated in the military, refers to a process where a prospective operation is critically reviewed by a select group of people with the intent of poking holes into its defenses, exposing risks and identifying all the ways a project might fail. By questioning every aspect of an operation, the evaluation results in either "killing" the idea or strengthening it.

The purpose of a murder board is not to attack the author of the operation; its goal is to develop a culture of contingency planning to determine what actions the group should take if things go wrong. "By analyzing where things are likely to fail, you're already preparing your countermeasures to pivot away from problems," says Hise.

When used in corporate settings, a murder board typically focuses on project management although it can be adapted for other uses. For the murder board session to be of value, Hise recommends the following:

- Choose board members who are experts on the topic being evaluated. The more members from different departments who can offer their viewpoints the better. Crucially, you want people who are curious and insightful versus unduly critical.

- Share example questions with board members ahead of time and ask them to prepare their own questions that are likely to uncover weak spots in the proposal.

- The person or team responsible for the idea should be reminded not to go on the defense—the exercise isn't a personal vendetta—but to instead offer up ideas as counterpoints.

- If everyone deems the project should continue, work these learnings into the proposal following the session.

"It's to your benefit to get into the mindset that your ideas need constant iteration," says Hise. "By assuming the worst, you bring out the best."

Assuming the worst to create a culture of contingency planning is equally important when it comes to a topic too often relegated to companies' IT departments—that of promoting cybersecurity.

6.5 Founder as "Chief Security Officer": Creating a Culture of Cybersecurity Resiliency

Keri Pearlson listened intently to renowned business leaders presenting at the featured session of the 2025 South by Southwest (SXSW) conference on what America's 33 million small businesses needed to do to prosper. One topic of particular interest to Keri never came up: cybersecurity. It wasn't the first time. At other business conferences and in other conversations with everyone from CEOs to founders, cybersecurity typically emerged as a secondary concern, if at all.

Keri is a principal research scientist at MIT Sloan whose research[8] on small to midsize companies has identified a false sense of security among their leadership. "The problem is, they think cybercriminals are targeting larger, well-established companies in part because these are the type of cyberattacks—the ones that impact an extensive customer base—that are covered by the media. They don't think of themselves as potential targets."

But Keri says their smaller size is often the very reason why they're targeted—in particular, small to medium-sized businesses that make up larger companies' supply chains are often viewed by cybercriminals as vectors to infect the systems of larger, harder-to-access companies.

One recent study cites that small businesses account for 43% of cyberattacks annually; a 46% of cyberattacks were against small businesses with 1,000 or fewer employees. On average, small and medium-sized businesses (SMBs) lose $25,000 due to cyberattacks. In 2020, small businesses faced more than 700,000 attacks, which caused a total of \$2.8 billion in damages.[9] Such damage can ultimately lead to failure.

According to Keri, the lack of attention to cybersecurity is exacerbated by a prevailing attitude that cybersecurity should be relegated to the IT department and a belief that AI can protect against all cyberattacks.

"An IT department can't keep an employee from clicking on a malicious link," says Keri. "And while AI promises to make it easier to identify malicious activity, you have to remember that the bad guys have AI, too. They're determined to find a way around just about any defense we create to stop them."

Because cybercriminals are always evolving their methods and techniques, Keri stresses the importance of building a cyber preventative and resilience culture. "Cybersecurity is everyone's issue, which is why it's so important for companies at all stages of growth to develop a cybersecurity culture as their first line of defense against cyber breaches."

Start-ups, Keri notes, hold an advantage in this area. Whereas processes may already be in place and habits formed at established companies, start-up founders have an opportunity to implement a cyber-savvy culture from the ground up.

To best protect your company, customers, employees and investors, founders need to assume the role of "chief security officer." According to Keri, here's how:

Create a Cybersecurity Crisis Communications Plan. The early stages of a cyber crisis are often chaotic with customers, partners, investors, and reporters, among others, demanding answers. By creating your plan in advance, you are better positioned to pivot and move quickly. Elements to consider in its creation are:

- How will you reach clients if your email is down?

- Which stakeholders will you need to contact?

- Who should you contact at your local and national law enforcement agencies? For example, do you know the number of your local FBI field office?

- If you lose your data, who do you contact, and who is responsible?

- Are there any responses you can craft in advance to use as a template in the event that reporters contact you?

Hold Fire Drills. Businesses regularly hold fire drills to ensure that work staff know what to do in the event of a fire or natural disaster. In a cyber-drill, simulate a cyberattack—case studies on cybersecurity breaches can help in this area—and have everyone act out their assigned roles. Then, simulate your step-by-step recovery.

Buy Cyber Insurance. Contact your insurance company to find out whether they offer any form of cyber insurance. If you don't, consider looking into cyber insurance policies to determine if it's worth the investment.

Back It Up "Old-School" Style. Keri's research uncovered a company that created a robust business continuity plan for a cyber crisis. But after they were hacked, no one was able to get online to access the plan.

As panic built, an administrative assistant clutching a folder approached her director. She asked, "Is this the plan?" Up until then, she'd been teased by colleagues about her habit of making hard copies of important documents. Now, she emerged as the company's hero.

Make it a habit to save key documents to a thumb drive, email them to yourself, and print them so you have multiple ways to access them in an emergency.

Reward "Cyber Heroes." Host a competition among your staff to see who can figure out real from fake links, documents, vendor invoices, and emails. This will help employees learn to pay attention to small irregularities like a minor misspelling in a website address or clues to identify an email's origins. Then reward those employees who do well.

Cybersecurity Moments. Keri once consulted on a cybersecurity plan with a bank in Brazil where the CEO would start every meeting with a "cybersecurity moment." These moments included his sharing media coverage on or social media posts about cybersecurity attacks, practices, and solutions.

"The CEO is sending the message that cybersecurity is something their business talks about," says Keri. "As chief security officer, you set the stage for building a cyber-savvy workforce."

6.6 Recessions: A Surprisingly Good Time to Launch a Start-Up

You've done the hard work of determining a solid product market fit, are intimate with your target market's pain point, and are comfortable with selling. You're on the brink of launching your start-up when the economy enters a recession. Your natural inclination is to hold back. According to a 2024 study by Daniel Bias of the Owen Graduate School of Management at Vanderbilt University and his co-author Alexander Ljungqvist of the Centre for Economic Policy Research (CEPR),[10] start-ups that launched during the Great Recession of 2008–2009 experienced substantially better long-term outcomes in terms of survival and growth in employment and sales.

These findings were further backed up in a 2025 *MIT Sloan Management Review* article by Steven H. Seggie, Berk Talay, and Koen Pauwels: on average, they found that new products launched during a recession have higher sales and market share and remain on the market longer than those launched during boom times. They also noted that launching later in the recession is better than earlier and that outcomes are better in severe recessions than middling ones, which they believe may be due to greater pent-up demand.[11]

Why is this? For starters, there's more affordable talent available during a recession due to corporate layoffs. This can help build a culture of frugality, which is critical for start-ups to survive. Office space is typically available at lower prices, further keeping overall expenses low. And if vendors' sales have been impacted, you are in a better position to negotiate with them. There's typically less competition, too, during this window of time. One example of a mega-company that launched during a recession is Microsoft during 1975s "Oil Shock" recession.[12]

But what about funding? "From the standpoint of a venture capital firm, recessions put downward pressure on private company valuations, which creates good value for venture firms to invest at low valuations," says Bill Kaiser, emeritus partner at Greylock Partners.

Some founders, too, realize that they can create value in a down market and wait for the economic cycle to improve to sell or go public.

So, while it may feel counterintuitive, entrepreneurs may be positioned to create a "competitive moat" when the economy is rocky by using deteriorating market conditions to their advantage.

Next, we'll meet an unlikely entrepreneur who launched two weeks before the 2020 COVID-19 lockdown. A meticulously thought-out marketing plan covering the span of one year was ripped up. It took a creative pivot to save the company.

Cara Nicoletti with her grandfather Seymour, the inspiration behind the name of her sausage brand.

Photo Credit: David Williams.

6.7 Cara Nicoletti, Seemore Meats & Veggies: Sausage Industry Disruptor

Cara Nicoletti's sinuses felt like they'd been pushed through a meat grinder. But that wasn't the worst of it. A sharp, stabbing pain in her ear was affecting her balance. All Cara wanted at that moment was to wrap herself up in a blanket and devour a bowl of chicken soup. But here she was instead on a floor crowded with men, meat, and machinery making long links of sausages.

"I didn't have health insurance," recalls Cara, 39, of the autumn day more than a decade ago that helped push her onto the path of launching her sustainable sausage business. "The owner of the meat cutting company where I worked told me it cost more to insure women. And since I was the only woman he employed, it would be my fault if I drove up all the men's premiums. I was so naïve I didn't question him. But that day was a turning point."

Back then Cara couldn't have envisioned she'd one day disrupt the business of sausage making by introducing a product that encouraged people to eat less meat. Launched in March 2020—two weeks before the COVID-19 lockdown—Seemore Meats & Veggies eschews the 98% meat content of traditional sausages by packing them with humanely raised quality meat thoughtfully paired with up to 35% of vegetables. These precooked, technicolored sausages—think bright reddish-pink and green among many other natural, veggie-induced shades—are free of antibiotics, nitrates, phosphate, and dyes and are higher in nutrients and lower in calories than traditional sausages. Popular options include cheesy breakfast hash, chicken kale pesto, chicken chili verde, and chicken parm sausages. Seemore Meats & Veggies products are currently on the shelves of 120 Target stores across the East Coast and are available on Cara's website, eatseemore.com.

"Even during the early days of launching Seemore, I didn't think of myself as an entrepreneur. I thought of myself as a butcher," says Cara.

The Smelly Room In 1929, Cara's great-grandfather Jack opened Salett's, a butcher shop in Boston's "Little Italy" located in the city's famed North End. Her beloved grandfather Seymour Salett, the inspiration behind the name of her sausages, later inherited the business. Cara was the only grandchild who wandered into what the family had dubbed the "smelly room."

"I was the curious one," she says. "I liked to peek behind the curtain to understand how the meat made it into the display case."

Seymour never planned to mentor family members. Butchery is hard, physical work and demands long hours. Precision is paramount in producing quality cuts and protecting fingers. Volume drives profit, and mom-and-pop shops like Seymour's can't compete in any meaningful way against the country's four major meat companies—Cargill Meat Solutions, Tyson Foods, JBS USA, and National Beef Packing—who control up to 85% of the hog, cattle, and chicken markets.[13] Meat money is hard earned money. Seymour did well enough to support his family and took pride in continuing the family business well into his 80s, but he was by no means a wealthy man.

Young Cara had quietly watched Seymour as he worked and memorized his techniques. When he learned that his granddaughter had grown passionate about the art and craft of butchery, he felt increasingly protective, telling Cara that he hoped her interest wouldn't stick.

With love and regret, Seymour would one day gift Cara with his butchery tools.

Stuffing Veggies into Sausages   Cara's early career path was far removed from entrepreneurship. A voracious reader of literary classics, Cara enrolled at New York University in 2004 to study English literature and Latin with the goal of becoming a professor. But when it came time to build a post-graduate résumé, she discovered internships involved unpaid labor. Cara quietly pushed thoughts of graduate school onto the back burner.

She stayed put in New York City, working first as a barista and then as a baker specializing in bread and pastries. During an offhand conversation at a restaurant where Cara was baking the owner shared that his grandfather, too, was a butcher—would Cara like to take on light butchery work breaking down pork shoulders and chickens when her baking slowed down after the holidays? As she worked with her grandfather's tools on her days off, something in her sparked. So, she visited butcher shops throughout Brooklyn to ask about apprenticeships and found one at the Meat Hook, which specialized in local meat from small, family-run farms.

Cara liked that the Meat Hooks' values aligned with hers—their beef was grass-fed and went from farm to family-owned slaughterhouses to their shop. Cara's relationship with meat had evolved into a larger vision—she wanted to widen access to the humane meat movement, particularly for those in lower economic brackets. There had to be a way, she reasoned, to satisfy consumers' cravings for meat while encouraging them to eat healthier. When the stacks of veggie burgers she positioned alongside lean beef and chicken weren't selling, she decided to stuff vegetables directly into the sausages. "I got some questioning looks, but I did it anyway," she says.

Cara's innovative approach solved two issues. A small operation, the Meat Hook struggled to keep up with consumer demand. By introducing vegetables into the sausages, she doubled their yield. Cara experimented with names that conjured up comfort—Chicken Soup and Chicken Parm Sausages were especially popular—and soon Cara's sausages were flying off the shelves. Nearly 4,500 pounds of meat[14] passed through her hands every week.

A Scalable Idea   While Cara's innovative approach to creating a healthier—and many would say, a tastier—sausage earned money for the businesses where she'd interned and worked, she hadn't pocketed any of the profits. Shoppers' enthusiasm showed there was a market, but how could she improve upon her offerings in anticipation of one day running her own business? The answer was closer than she thought.

Cara and Aaron Foster first bonded over a shared love of cheese. His former workplace was housed in the same building as the Meat Hook, and they had often crossed paths. In 2015, Aaron launched Foster Sundry, a specialty grocery shop in Brooklyn. He wanted to introduce whole-animal butchery as well, and the first person who came to mind was Cara.

"Aaron encouraged experimentation," says Cara. "He enabled me to explore interesting combinations of vegetables and meats along with gauging customer feedback."

Gooey cheese, roasted tomatoes, basil, kale, caramelized onions, carrots, celery, and buttery baked potatoes found their way into various sausages with names such as Bubbe's Chicken Soup, Broccoli Melt, Chicken Parm, and La Dolce Beet-a. Once again, Cara's sausages flew off the shelves. She continued to fine-tune her recipes—some of which Foster Sundry uses to this day—until she felt ready to strike out on her own, with Aaron's blessing.

But Cara quickly learned that due to USDA regulations there would be restrictions—if she opened a butchery shop in New York, it meant she could only sell products within the state, and she would need to access a licensed facility if she planned to make sausages by hand.[15] Cara reached out to business owners she'd met through the Brooklyn food scene for their insights. Erin Patinkin, founder of the popular bakery chain Ovenly, did not mince words. "Don't open a shop," she advised.

"If I was going to influence as many people as possible to eat healthier and more humanely, I'd need to mass market my product," says Cara. "And Erin recommended I embrace what I loved and did best—creating my own sausage brand," says Cara.

Erin liked Cara's idea and went on to become a co-founder of what they called, through a play on words, Seemore Meats & Veggies in honor of Cara's beloved mentor Papa Seymour.

"Because 35% of our fillings are vegetables, the USDA wouldn't allow us to use the word *sausages* on our packaging," says Cara. "But we fought against the ruling and won." But for reasons that remain unknown to Cara, they weren't allowed to use the word "vegetables," so they've opted for "veggies" on the packaging instead.

Erin helped demystify funding and set the stage for the start-up to scale. She also introduced Cara to another future co-founder, Ariel Hauptman, who specialized in operations, marketing, branding, and sales.[16] When it came to designing a logo and packaging, the women opted for a nonpretentious, clean look to appeal to an array of shoppers. The color of each package's hand-drawn sausages reflected the color of the meat-veggie combo being sold.

With a smart, savvy, and talented team coming together, the hard work of launching their new brand was just beginning.

Refusing to Accept No as an Answer   Sausages are a bound meat. Sausages stuffed with two-thirds of vegetables are scientifically difficult to make because the veggies contain water, which is the enemy of protein extraction, making them difficult to bind. Cara knew if her start-up was to scale, she'd need the assistance of a co-packing company to cook, process, and blend the meat and vegetables together. She expected it to be a hard sell, and she was right.

Seemore Meats & Veggies was rejected by 100 co-packing companies before Paradise Locker Meats expressed interest in working with her. Cara then spent two years finding meat suppliers who were certified by the Global Animal Partnership, which is one of the largest animal welfare food labeling programs in North America, and small farms who grew quality, organic vegetables. "We were determined to work with companies that care about sustainability and treat their employees well," she says.

Seemore Meat & Veggies was incorporated in 2019 with the goal of securing adequate investment funding to launch onto shelves in 2020. Their biggest rivals were plant-based meat and alternative protein products, which raised $235 million in Q1 2025, bringing total investments since 2016 to $18.6 billion.[17] The pressure was on.

"Our earliest funders didn't know much about meat," says Cara. "They were simply having fun diversifying their investment portfolios. Most importantly, they believed our product was scalable."

When it came to determining the pricing of Seemore Meats & Veggie, Cara, like her grandfather before her, needed to work within the pricing parameters set by Cargill Meat Solutions, Tyson Foods, JBS USA, and National Beef Packing, the country's meat conglomerates. Overhead—including purchases from farms, co-packing, production, shipping, packaging, staffing, and marketing—gobbled up funds, so Cara and her co-founders courted investors in Series Seed rounds.

To their delight, Seemore Meats & Veggies began to pique the interest of grocery chains. Cara took this as a good omen and felt confident about launching Seemore Meats & Veggies in March 2020.

COVID Speed Bump   Food samples in little white cups lined up in neat rows and distributed by a company rep to grocery shoppers were a popular treat at supermarkets across the country before COVID-19 was declared a pandemic a mere two weeks after Seemore launched. Cara was counting on the sausages' bright colors, the sizzling sound and smell of them cooking on supermarkets' mini-grills, and conversations about a healthier and more humane option to traditional sausages to grow a loyal customer base.

Trade shows, too, which attract new corporate buyers, were put on hold indefinitely. Other problems arose. The pandemic hit the country's meat supply along with its supply chain,[18] with empty grocery shelves and panic buying infiltrating supermarkets nationwide.

"Our entire marketing launch was based on live events," says Cara. "Out of necessity, we tore up a full year of planning and pivoted."[19]

First, they built an entirely new website on Shopify so customers could seamlessly order sausages online. That, strengthened with a dedicated email strategy and daily postings on Instagram, helped create momentum. The co-founders and their marketing team shipped sausages to as many family members, friends, and friends of friends that they could think of, which translated into people posting colorful pictures and testimonies online.

"Key to our success was leading with humor and working hard to educate consumers in the most approachable way to drive home our message—Seemore is about quality meat and veggies, together."

As the pandemic roared, billboards in Los Angeles and New York City became more affordable, leading to larger-than-life images of Seemore sausages in two key markets. They tapped into meme culture, created and sold sausage-forward merchandise, and utilized online networks like SocialNature, an app that lets you try full-size samples in exchange for honest reviews.

They also ramped up merchandising efforts, worked on multiple instant redeemable coupon campaigns to entice people to make purchases, along with experimenting with different designs to capture consumers' attention.

"Building a talented and creative marketing team that could pivot when faced with adversity made all the difference," says Cara.

Seemore, Make More   Despite its debut in the shadow of COVID-19 pandemic, Seemore Meats & Veggies has earned $6 million in sales since its launch in 2020. Investors remain enthusiastic about the company's scaling up and growth potential. Cara takes pride in leading a start-up that is carbon-neutral, uses packaging created with an eye toward sustainability, and continues to value the entire ecosystem of food production. And her beloved Papa and product namesake Seymour, now in his 90s, remains one of Cara's most enthusiastic cheerleaders. Her fiancé, too, reminds her to slow down and take a moment to bask in her accomplishments.

"I never in my life thought I'd have financial stability," says Cara. "While I miss working with my hands, I love working with the people helping us to make the product and embracing the creative marketing side of the business where I'm building out the visual tone of the brand." Cara smiles, "And I now have good health insurance, too."

7

Endings and Beginnings

7.1 Age and High-Growth Entrepreneurship

Entrepreneurship is often associated with youth, a notion strengthened by the wild success of super founders like Bill Gates who was 20 years old when he co-founded Microsoft, and Mark Zuckerberg who launched Facebook from his Harvard dorm room at the age of 19 before dropping out. But is this really the norm in the tech sector and beyond?

No, according to a research paper co-authored by MIT Sloan Professor Pierre Azoulay. In "Age and High-Growth Entrepreneurship,"[1] published in the journal *American Economics Review: Insights*, he and a team of co-researchers studied start-ups systematically in the United States, integrating administrative data on firms, workers, and owners, and found that the average age of entrepreneurs at the time they founded their companies was 42, with the vast majority running small businesses. In software start-ups, a field most often associated with young founders, the average age was 40. The age range rose even higher in industries like oil and gas or biotechnology, hovering around 47.

But what about the most successful start-ups? Professor Azoulay and his co-authors dug deep into the data and found that among the top 0.1% of start-ups based on growth in their first five years, the founders started their companies, on average, at 45 years old.[2]

Their findings point to older entrepreneurs having more access to greater human capital, social capital, or financial capital. That, and mastery takes time.

So, while journeying into one's 50s is most often met with a desire to wind down one's career, others—like the two entrepreneurs we'll meet next—view it as a springboard into a new beginning.

7.2 Entrepreneurship as a Second Act: Dave Picarillo, Twin Barns Brewing Company

Wouldn't it be nice to be an entrepreneur?

For Dave Picarillo, launching his own business was a lingering thought that popped up here and there between corporate meetings, providing for his family, and catching weekly early morning flights between Topco Associate's Boston and Chicago offices where the longtime consultant worked for 13 years. In those rare quiet moments Dave would imagine taking his favorite hobby—brewing beer—and building a business around it with a scenic vacation setting as its backdrop. But then he was on to his next meeting or flight and the dream would fade into the background.

"It felt like the stars never quite aligned," says Dave. "I faced financial pressures and personal responsibilities, and for a long

Cheers! Brewed at Twin Barns Brewing Company.
Photo Credit: Dave Picarillo.

time I never acted on my entrepreneurial impulse. Launching a business felt too risky and intimidating."

Dave discovered home brewing during his undergraduate years at Worcester Polytechnic Institute. It bridged two of his passions: engineering, which was the focus of his undergraduate degree, and a growing interest in beer.

"In creating recipes, brewing involves chemistry, physics, and biology," says Dave. "By experimenting you find out which malts interact best with certain hops and yeasts. I remain fascinated with the whole brewing process. It's equal parts art and mad scientist."

Dave's interests extended beyond the beer itself. "I was curious about the stories behind a name chosen for a craft beer, the taverns that served them, and the brewers creating them," he says.

While immersed in growing his career, Dave made a point to seek out local breweries wherever his corporate travels took him. Likewise, breweries were his top destination for hosting staff and personal gatherings. Sometimes his friends or family would shake their heads at the thought of venturing to yet another brewery (especially his wife). But one person in his life who needed no persuading was his good friend Bruce Walton. The two had spent many evenings over the course of their 25-year friendship knocking back a few cold ones or delighting in the discovery of new craft beers while joking about how they'd one day launch their own brewery.

It wasn't until Dave was in his early 50s that an opportunity to scratch the entrepreneurial itch presented itself. Topco Associates was restructuring, and Dave decided it was a good time to retire. He weighed options for his next act. Around that same time, he and Bruce embarked on a two-day brewery tour. The topic of launching their own brewery weaved in and out of their conversations. Dave was now retired, and Bruce, a fellow consultant, felt worn down by the constant travel and was considering doing the same. Both had money in the bank and adult children embarking on their own careers. They agreed, too, that their life experiences had taught them how to better manage risk.

Late that Saturday evening over two Treehouse New England IPAs, the two decided, "Let's just do it."

Renovating the Old, Tired Barns   As Dave toured the old, sad-looking twin barns in New Hampshire's lakes region, his stomach sank. Two construction companies had passed on renovating the structures, fearing they were beyond help. "My thought process was along the lines of, *My God, what have we done?*" recalls Dave.

The purchase of the property was the culmination of two years of work on Dave and Bruce's part. The duo had written a detailed business plan that helped them capture the feel and look of the brewery business they aimed to build, one that would include a restaurant, bar, live music, and an outside entertainment area. In terms of securing finance, they first approached larger banks but discovered their brewing operation was deemed too small, so they opted to borrow from a smaller, local bank. They had narrowed down their choice of locations and diligently researched gaps in food and beverage services in towns bordering Lake Winnipesaukee, which, at 21 miles long, is New Hampshire's largest lake and a popular vacation destination where competition was fierce in snapping up prime pieces of real estate.

During a brewery tour in 2017, Dave and Bruce stumbled across what at first appeared to be one old barn in Meredith, New Hampshire. Built in 1850, they discovered the tired looking structure that housed a gaggle of abandoned mannequins and motorcycles—where they came from, no one was sure—consisted of two barns joined together on seven acres of farmland. The partners immediately saw its potential. And while the two earlier construction companies passed on the renovation project, a construction engineer they consulted felt otherwise. "He told us he initially thought he was going to destroy our dream, but upon further inspection he deemed the shape of the barns as 'not that bad,'" recalls Dave.

Building Community   Dave and Bruce traded in their ties and suits for jeans and work boots and joined in on tearing down and building new walls. "We viewed the property through the lens of wanting to create a sense of community," says Dave. The menu paired fine crafted beer with pub food. Warm shades of wood, communal tables, and games like cornhole, a ring toss, ping-pong, and an oversized version of Connect Four were meant to be inviting to adults and children alike. "We invested in comfortable Adirondack chairs inside and outside the barns to give it a 'sitting around the campfire' feel."

Twin Barns Brewing Company opened its doors in July 2019 to enthusiastic throngs of tourists and locals. "Bruce and I brewed *a lot* of beer that first year," says Dave. "We always kept four beers on tap including a New England IPA, blonde ale, a dark beer, and a pilsner. The other eight taps were for experimenting with new and old beers, knowing we could always go back to something customers really liked. A taster panel with beers ranging from light to dark was a popular way to sample."

They also introduced a beer school for waitstaff so they could speak knowledgeably when beer questions came up. "It's also a mini-history class, too, with a nod to the town's flagship IPAs. Our Palmerstown Pub ale is the original name of the town of Meredith. The dunkel beer we serve is the same beer that was served the first year of Munich's Oktoberfest."

The partners also took turns working every job responsible for maintaining Twin Barns including bar tending, waiting tables, brewing, maintenance, finance, marketing, bookkeeping, and operations to gain crucial insights and experience into the customer experience. "We wanted to be smart about answering any questions that came up before handing off positions," says Dave.

As part of their marketing efforts Dave invested hours into what he jokingly called "beer pornography"—using lighting and backdrops to create attractive images of beer. An equal amount of thought and attention went into the captions. He was proud of the results, but they garnered only a small amount of views and likes. Then he tried posting candid photos of dogs visiting Twin Barns with their owners. To his and Bruce's surprise, the shots immediately went viral. "It taught me that our commitment to building community extended into our marketing efforts," says Dave. "We rarely take photos of stand-alone beer now. People enjoying our beer, children and adults playing, beloved pets—they make people want to join in on the fun."

The partners were caught off-guard when COVID-19 protocols were put in place. But come summer, their seven acres of land and earlier investment in community-building and entertainment—and a new beer garden built over the winter for outdoor dining—helped them thrive during a time when some restaurants were closing down.

Today, Twin Barns continues to thrive. When business drops off after Columbus Day, Dave and Bruce turn their attention to their second brewery, Twin Barns North, which they launched in New Woodstock, a popular ski resort town in northern New Hampshire.

"Coming from the corporate world, I've since developed a deep respect for entrepreneurs. Because even when you aren't physically at your company, you're thinking about it. You're responsible for every aspect of the business including for your staff's livelihood and you don't want to let them down," says Dave.

So, would he do it all over again? "In a heartbeat." "Co-owning Twin Barns is by far the best job I've ever had. We now wish we'd launched it sooner."

The one thing that hasn't changed? "Bruce and I still regularly visit other breweries. We're always open to trying something new."

7.3 Charlie Tillinghast: From MSNBC.com President to Founder of Factal

In 2005, Charlie Tillinghast was named president and CEO of MSNBC Interactive News, a joint venture launched by Microsoft and NBC News nine years earlier. Leading up to his promotion, Charlie had worked as MSNBC Interactive News' publisher and general manager and, earlier, as director of sales & business, positions that provided him with insight into the online news site's business model and content creation. He witnessed the online news site's ascent during the dot-com boom propelled by interactive storytelling, sleek video productions, and other robust multimedia offerings. By 2012, MSNBC.com would yield $120 million in revenue with a 25% net profit margin and 300 employees stationed across the globe.

MSNBC-TV, meanwhile, was struggling to find its footing against CNN and an emergent Fox News. Both MSNBC entities had been positioned as impartial news services in the traditional model of broadcast news and top-tier newspapers. Charlie was committed to upholding the online news outlet's impartiality, one devoid of opinion columns or similar opinionated content. But within the broadcast division, leadership was reconsidering this stance.

In 2006, Microsoft divested its interest, but the name MSNBC remained the same. Soon after, MSNBC-TV began to gain market traction by introducing a liberal opinion format that differentiated it from ratings leader Fox News. This move made business sense for MSNBC-TV, which had up to that point lacked a strong brand identity. But it created brand perception problems for MSNBC.com, which continued to deliver an impartial news product. The *New York Times* reported[3] on a leaked company memo in which Charlie was cited as saying, "Both strategies are fine, but naming them the same thing is brand insanity." Regardless, NBC News dismissed creating two separate brands.

Charlie and his editorial team turned their attention to leveraging news brands within the NBC family to create standalone sites that included *Today*, *Meet-the-Press*, *Nightly News*, and the *Maddow Blog* to appeal to multiple market segments beyond audiences consuming general, impartial news. Most significantly, Charlie and his team acquired @BreakingNews in 2009 and launched a stand-alone start-up within the NBC News corporation.

An Intrapreneurial-Inspired Start-Up

Charlie's acquisition of @BreakingNews is an example of intrapreneurial behavior, which mimics the characteristics of entrepreneurs—inventive, innovative, forward-thinking—except it plays out within the structures of well-established companies.

"A lot of times people believe that entrepreneurship is strictly associated with start-ups; that's not how we look at it," said Bill Aulet, managing director of the Martin Trust Center for MIT Entrepreneurship in an interview with MIT Sloan's *Ideas Made to Matter*.[4] "We believe that entrepreneurship is a way of creating value with new products, new ways of running businesses, and with a number of assets that you control. But also assets that you don't control. So, entrepreneurs can exist in corporations, and corporations need them more and more."

BreakingNews debuted as a Twitter account launched by Michael Van Poppel, a 20-year-old Netherlands resident who relied on Twitter feeds to detect newsworthy events, a new approach that proved to be a faster and more effective way of identifying breaking stories than traditional methods used by established news outlets. With its speed and agility, BreakingNews attracted an audience of around one million followers. This caught Charlie's attention—he recognized that the shift to social media and mobile news gathering would bring profound changes to the future of identifying and distributing breaking news. He wisely negotiated the acquisition of @breakingnews followed by the purchase of the BreakingNews.com URL. Then, he formed a team to build algorithms to detect breaking news stories even faster, primarily through multiple social media channels. Charlie appointed Cory Bergman head of product and Ben Tesch to head up technology and assembled an editorial team led by veteran journalist Tom Brew to verify facts and sources and compose updates linked to their original sources. The site's popularity grew rapidly, particularly among government agencies and corporations.

"The White House Situation Room displayed BreakingNews on its wall monitors," says Charlie. "Former Senator John McCain shared that it was his favorite app."[5]

Corporate risk intelligence analysts increasingly relied on BreakingNews as well for updates on dangerous, impactful events such as earthquakes, tsunamis, terrorist attacks, or plane crashes, among many others. BreakingNews was the first to report in 2016 on the Bastille Day terrorist attack in Nice, France,[6] that killed 86 people based on tips submitted by users of the app.

But issues arose out of its success—the MSNBC online newsroom didn't like being scooped by BreakingNews. Neither did NBC News' editorial team. Charlie was able to provide cover for BreakingNews to freely innovate without internecine interference.

In 2012, Microsoft sold its share of the MSNBC News Interactive venture to NBC News, which prioritized increasing its broadcast ratings. Charlie felt it was a good time to leave MSNBC and transition into a new leadership position at a media technology company. He continued to follow BreakingNews' progress.

As 2016 wound down, Charlie was alarmed to read a blog post from his BreakingNews co-founder Cory Bergman that NBC News was shutting down the entire operation. The nature of BreakingNews content—accidents, terrorism, and shootings—had proven not to be particularly appealing to brand advertisers. But Cory shared with Charlie that his proposal to create a paid-subscription service for BreakingNews had been rejected by management. In the end, NBC News chose not to solicit buyout offers despite BreakingNews' robust audience of more than 10 million Twitter followers and a large base of app users.

"I couldn't believe NBC was shutting down a perfectly good business, one that had proven its ability to fulfill a need for gathering crucial, verified news data," says Charlie. The market felt the same way as evidenced from the inordinate amount of emails filling Cory's inbox from stunned individuals, corporations, newsrooms, nongovernmental organizations (NGOs), and other organizations around the world that relied on BreakingNews.

While reflecting on its shuttering, Charlie realized how much he'd enjoyed growing a new business within MSNBC and the autonomy it allowed him to innovate within the news industry. He recognized, too, that BreakingNews' closure created an opportunity to offer a similar service, one he felt qualified to lead. But could a similar news operation be reproduced without using NBC News' intellectual property? Yes, Cory assured him.

Now in his mid-50s, Charlie, a former president and CEO, was invited by Cory and Ben to join them as a co-founder of the successor to BreakingNews. With proven product know-how and existing demand, the ingredients for a successful start-up were clear. "There's a misconception that entrepreneurs thrive on risk-taking when, in actuality, smart entrepreneurs work hard to eliminate risk," says Charlie.

The Launch of Factal.com

In 2018, Charlie invested the first seed capital in the start-up, which he co-named Factal to connote a news and data gathering organization committed to impartial, fact-based reporting. But rather than positioning Factal as a general news organization, the founders exclusively focused on providing what BreakingNews' most ardent followers signaled they needed the most: verified risk intelligence.

"Let's face it—threats can come from anywhere at any time," says Charlie. "When critical events are unfolding, a deluge of data can hamper companies' and agencies' ability to make the quick, concise decisions necessary to protect their people and assets around the globe."

The Factal founders created a risk intelligence platform for online and mobile use, bringing together global risk intelligence, threat detection, and corporate brand monitoring. And while algorithms drive data collection across social media and news sites, discerning humans—many of which are former BreakingNews editors and journalists—make sense of the daily jumble of data from which they construct the most timely, impactful, and verified news updates for their users around the globe. And in what Factal touts as an industry first, the platform connects members in security, crisis, and risk teams in a secure chat to collaborate around global events.

Charlie and the founders spent the early months before their launch running beta testing with Fortune 500 companies that had previously relied on BreakingNews, which helped them perfect their product and land their first customers. The beta testing led to their raising sufficient seed capital from angel investors. To provide around-the-clock service, Factal opened a London newsroom staffed by multilingual journalists with expertise working in many world regions.

"We introduced the tagline 'from the founders of BreakingNews', which provided us with the type of market awareness—and a way to connect with former BreakingNews clients—that few start-ups enjoy. Trade shows, in-bound and outbound inquiries, and word-of-mouth further grew our client base."

For their business model, Factal opted for a one-year flat fee subscription with the option to purchase advanced capabilities. Today, Factal is profitable and growing quickly with hundreds of corporations, government agencies, and NGOs as subscribers. As part of their mission, humanitarian relief organizations including Team Rubicon, Direct Relief, and World Central Kitchen have access to Factal for free and rely on the platform to help people impacted by hurricanes, earthquakes, and outbreaks around the globe.

"While BreakingNews was designed for the social media age, we built Factal for the mis- and disinformation age," says Charlie.

"There's no higher urgency to get the facts right than when a breaking news event puts people at risk."

7.4 The Challenges of Letting Go

Regardless of what age founders embark on their entrepreneurial journey, there comes a time when an exit ramp looks increasingly attractive. However, some founders keep on driving rather than letting go of the steering wheel, even if it ends up hurting their company in the long run.

Bob Brennan once served as CEO of Iron Mountain[7] (NYSE:IRM), a company he helped grow into one of the largest storage and information management services in the world servicing more than 225,000 organizations, 95% of which were Fortune 1,000 companies. Now, years after stepping down from his leadership position, he quips, "It's not a long way from 'there goes Bob Brennan' to 'who's Bob Brennan?'"

While Bob's comment shows a keen level of self-awareness and a sense of humor about transitioning out of a position of influence, this sentiment often underpins why some entrepreneurs hold onto their company well after it makes sense to sell or step into a supportive role under new ownership. Because entrepreneurs often overcome great odds to found and grow great companies, it's no surprise they have a hard time letting go—after all, it's their "baby." No one else, they may reason, truly understands the ins and outs of running the company at scale. But often, there's another element at play: the level of commitment involved in growing a company may result in over-identifying with the leadership role. If you're not grounded, *I am the founder* is a few steps away from *who am I beyond being the founder?* It's important to avoid the temptation of making the company your identity.

7.5 Selling Your Company: Best Practices

While selling your company may bring up a range of complex emotions, you don't want emotion driving the process. Think clearly about what you want before moving forward. Here are some best practices:

- **Begin with the end in mind.** Entrepreneurs sell a lot more than just their company. Everything created within this space is up for sale: the product, intellectual property, brand, work culture, customer contact information, and reputation. This is why it's so important to start your entrepreneurial journey with the end in mind. By mastering each topic we've explored and dissected in this book, you better position yourself for a strong finish. In particular, by assuming the role of chief salesperson, you will hone active listening skills to better understand what potential buyers need and have more experience in negotiation tactics, which will go a long way in setting yourself up for a premium exit.

- **Market your company's scarcity value.** It's important to differentiate your company from other competitors looking to sell. Emphasize to potential buyers not only your product's unique features but also the depth of your customer relationships and the breadth and maturity of your employees.

- **Understand the realities of your ownership stake.** If you own 100% of your company, the decision for price and terms is yours alone. If you own less than 50% of the company, your board of directors—most often comprised of investors and independent directors—must vote on the decision to sell and at what price. The sales skills you've honed over the years will come in handy if you need to convince your investors that it's the right time to sell. Be aware that it may take compromise to reach a deal.

- **"Sell" your workplace culture.** According to Tom Bogan, former CEO of Adaptive Insights and former vice chairman of Workday, "Culture is the single most important determinant of success or failure when large companies acquire smaller companies. Acquiring companies consider a startup's culture as much as they look at product strategy and sales growth when considering an acquisition." In short, acquirers want to know if the prospect company's employees will enjoy working for them and buy into their company's mission and culture. Even if product synergies are strong, if there is a cultural mismatch, the acquisition will fail.

- **Learn how the acquisition process works.** If you are being acquired by a larger company, be aware that each company acquisition is a unique transaction. For example, an acquirer may offer to pay you cash or company stock for your business or an "earn out" where you get paid over a predetermined period of time. A deal like this is likely to have performance conditions that the acquired company must meet for you to receive payment. The acquirer may also require you to remain at your company for a certain period.

- **Fix your problems.** Potential buyers do not want to inherit a company's problems. It's imperative to improve areas where a company is underperforming before attempting to sell. If it's evident that your sales are slowing down or your product needs upgrading or your work culture is subpar, you may inadvertently signal that you *must* sell. This puts buyers in a better position to negotiate and drive down your asking price.

Ideally, you want buyers to approach *you* about selling your company. If it's thriving, buyers will offer a higher price than if you put the company on the market or sell through a broker. In essence, great companies are bought, not sold.

7.6 Cementing Your Legacy

In some cases, it can be incredibly productive for founders to stay with the company they founded after going public or being sold by moving into a less central role. Bill Gates from Microsoft, Larry Ellison from Oracle, and Michael Dell from Dell Computer are good examples.

Bill Warner, whom we met in Chapter 1, did just this when he hired Curt Rawley as the new CEO who subsequently oversaw Avid's explosive growth and public offering. Bill recognized that the success of his company was more important than remaining as CEO. This further enabled around one dozen early Avid employees to assume the roles of CEOs at a wide range of companies. These CEOs learned "what good looked like" at Avid and were motivated and equipped to repeat the experience, which is a legacy in itself.

Bill Warner has forever changed the way we edit film and video, but his legacy extends well beyond this incredible feat. Bill is the president and founder of Co-Flow Investing, LLC, his entity for direct investing in early-stage entrepreneurs using solely his own personal investments. He serves as an investor and mentor at TechStars Boston, a national start-up accelerator that began in Boulder, Colorado, and has expanded to Boston, Seattle, and New York City. In his role as an advisor and mentor in the Gordon-MIT Engineering Leadership Program, he helps engineering students in developing leadership skills. He also serves as president at Move With Freedom, a nonprofit he co-founded that designs advanced mobility devices and makes those designs open source so manufacturers can bring them to market.

Liz Elting, whom we met in our sales chapter, achieved a premium exit when she sold her company Transperfect, the world's largest provider of language services. She has thrived in the role of philanthropist, launching the Elizabeth Elting

Foundation whose mission is to promote progressive and feminist efforts to eradicate systemic barriers, promote public health and education, achieve workplace equality, rise beyond the glass ceiling, and open the doors to economic independence for those society has far too often shut out. Says Liz, "I was raised to take initiative and work to make the world a better and more interconnected place. That has been the guiding force and common thread throughout my career."[8]

7.7 Why Entrepreneurs Endure

"Anyone speaking on a conference panel who makes entrepreneurship sound easy is full of shit," says Murli Thirumale. "You're creating something out of nothing—there's no product, brand, or customer. In most cases, all you have is passion and an untested idea. The entrepreneurial journey is a challenging journey."

Murli, 64, should know. A serial entrepreneur with deep roots in Silicon Valley, he founded three companies—Net6, Ocarina Networks, and Portworx—all of which he sold for a premium exit. "There were challenges during various stages of my companies' growth when I felt like I'd wandered into one of the circles of hell in *Dante's Inferno*."

So why do it? Why not stay in a comfortable position where you're guaranteed health insurance and paid vacation/sick leave? Murli could have chosen not to veer off this path. Early in his career, he served as a general manager at Hewlett-Packard and was named vice president and general manager of Symmetricon, a company that specialized in high-precision timekeeping technology. His environment was highly structured. He wasn't responsible for every single aspect of growing a company. Why take on so much risk?

"Because the flip side is pure magic," says Murli. "You're creating something out of nothing, and you experience the joy of people buying products and services from a company you invented for the betterment of their lives. Entrepreneurship brings freedom and a sense of fulfillment. It's truly a natural high."

But entrepreneurs end up creating more than just companies. "A company's leadership style is reflected in its work culture, and that work culture becomes as much of an entity as the company's products—it becomes a living thing."

Murli is an advocate of creating a positive work culture, which he believes gives start-ups a competitive advantage. "Yes, there are jerks who become wildly successful. But you don't have to systematically chew up and spit out people on your way to the top. It's to your advantage to build loyalty. By bringing the best out of people you build your competitive edge and cement your legacy."

One of the things Murli is most proud of is having passed what he calls the "supermarket test." "When a former employee sees you out grocery shopping, do they come up and shake your hand, or do you glimpse them out of the corner of your eye slinking around an aisle or ducking behind a display? Let me tell you, the first scenario is much more satisfying."

The time and energy Murli invested in the work culture of his three companies came to fruition during his retirement party in March 2025. "I learned that 13 start-ups were created by former employees. To me, this is a legacy in and of itself."

■ ■ ■

We hope this book provides you with the tools you need to knock down the walls of your comfort zone and embark on the journey of a lifetime. Why take the risk? Because what you create as an entrepreneur has the potential to live on after you. Entrepreneurship is a gift that you give to yourself.

Further Readings

We've referenced authors throughout our book and have listed their books here for further reading along with other books that have inspired us:

- *Aligning Strategy and Sales: The Choices, Systems, and Behaviors That Drive Effective Selling* by Frank V. Cespedes
- *Competing Against Luck: The Story of Innovation and Customer Choice* by Clayton Chirstenson
- *Disciplined Entrepreneurship: 24 Steps to a Successful Startup* by Bill Aulet
- *Dream Big and Win: Translating Passion into Purpose and Creating a Billion Dollar Business* by Liz Elting
- *The Entrepreneur Mind: 100 Essential Beliefs, Characteristics, and Habits of Elite Entrepreneurs* by Kevin D. Johnson
- *Entrepreneurship: Choice and Strategy* by Joshua Gans and Erin Scott
- *The Experimentation Machine: Finding Product-Market Fit in the Age of AI* by Jeff Bussgang
- *Going There* by Katie Couric
- *The Lean Startup: How Today's Entrepreneurs Use Continuous Innovation to Create Radically Successful Businesses* by Eric Ries

- *The Media Training Bible: 101 Things You Absolutely, Positively Need to Know Before Your Next Interview* by Brad Phillips
- *MIT Sloan's Ideas Made to Matter* at https://mitsloan.mit .edu/ideas-made-to-matter
- *The Mom Test: How to Talk to Customers & Learn If Your Business Is a Good Idea When Everyone Is Lying to You* by Rob Fitzpatrick
- *Sailing True North, Ten Admirals and the Voyage of Character* by Admiral James Stavridis
- *Sales Acceleration Formula: Using Data, Technology, and Inbound Selling to Go from $0 to $100 Million* by Mark Roberge
- *There's Got to Be a Better Way: How to Deliver Results and get rid of the Stuff That Gets in the Way of Real Work* by Donald C. Kieffer and Nelson Repenning
- *Think Again: The Power of Knowing What You Don't Know* by Adam Grant
- *Why Startups Fail: A New Roadmap for Entrepreneurial Success* by Tom Eisenmann
- *Zero to One: Notes on Startups, or How to Build the Future* by Peter Thiel

Disclosures

I have worked with the following companies named in this book as either an investor or an advisor and have equity interest in them:

- Factal
- Katie Couric Media
- Seemore Meats & Veggies
- Spoiler Alert
- Titan Casket
- Twin Barns
- WayScript

I have made a charitable donation to Eight Million Stories.

—Lou Shipley

Acknowledgments

Lou and Patricia

We are grateful to the entrepreneurs who entrusted us with telling their inspiring stories: Ricky Ashenfelter, Mason Barret, Katie Couric, Liz Elting, Scott Ginsberg, Jason Lieblich, Emily Malina, Mary McLaughlin, John Molner, Carl Mönefors, Cara Nicoletti, Dave Picarillo, Marvin Pierre, Errico Porzio, Matthew Riley, Murlie Thurimale, Charlie Tillinghast, and Bill Warner.

Many thanks to the experts whose insights have played a vital role in our storytelling: Debora Ancona, Bill Aulet, Pierre Azoulay, Elise Bates, Tom Bogan, Bob Brennan, Gina Carr, Frank Cespedes, Jake Cook, Mark Fusco, Hise Gibson, Michelle Goodwin, Bill Kaiser, Will Keller, Rob Ketterson, Lily Lyman, Tom Ohanian, Keri Pearlson, Brad Phillips, Mark Roberge, and Francisco Shiavone.

Our sincere thanks to the talented team at Wiley for guiding us through the publishing process: Trinity Crompton, Purvi Patel, Jeanenne Ray, Victoria Savahn, Adaobi Obi Tulton and Kim Wimpsett.

Special thanks to Mark Roberge and Liz Elting for introducing us to Wiley and to Linda Joffee Hull for helping us early on when we were initially putting our book idea together.

Lou

I would like to thank Patricia for asking me to join her on this journey. And a special thanks to my wife, Amanda, and my children, Clarke, Caroline, and Vanessa, for their endless editing and brainstorming.

Thanks all the Harvard Business School and MIT Sloan students I have had the privilege to teach.

And a special appreciation to Bill Warner and Curt Rawley for believing that I could make a difference at Avid. It was my first start-up, and it changed my life.

Patricia

Thank you, Lou, for your insights and wisdom throughout this writing journey.

Many thanks to my husband, David, and my daughter, Lily, for supporting my work-life-write balancing act while completing this book. It was quite a challenge, and I couldn't have done it without your support.

To all the MIT Sloan students and alumni entrepreneurs I've had the privilege of working with over my two decades at MIT Sloan—I remain in awe of your intelligence, innovation, work ethic, and drive. Your principled leadership makes the world a better place.

Thank you to the MIT Sloan academics studying and teaching entrepreneurship—I've learned so much from you.

To my colleagues in the MIT Sloan Office of Communications—thank you so much for your support of and enthusiasm for the book with a special shout-out to Amy MacMillan Bankson, Casey Bayer, Matthew Aliberti, Joe Higgins, and Kate O'Sullivan.

Many thanks to my readers Matthew Greif and Jennifer Fuchel for your friendship and insightful editorial suggestions. Thank you, too, to Felicia Sinusas for editorial insights shared.

To my mother for her constant support, and in memory of my father, Roland, and sister, Karen.

Thank you to my MFA mentor William Lychak—you were a guiding force while completing my degree. And to Garrard Conley and my classmates at the Fine Arts Work Center—thanks for your constructive criticism of and enthusiasm for my earliest unlikely entrepreneur profiles.

Lastly, thanks to all the baristas who kept me properly caffeinated.

Notes

Introduction

1. Virgin Media O2 Press Release, "Virgin Media O2 and Daisy Group Announce New B2B Company to Create Communications and IT Powerhouse for UK Businesses," May 12, 2025; https://news.virginmediao2.co.uk/virgin-media-o2-and-daisy-group-announce-new-b2b-company-to-create-communications-and-it-powerhouse-for-uk-businesses/
2. National Inventors Hall of Fame, William J. Warner, Digital Nonlinear Editing System, U.S. Patent No. 4,970,663; https://www.invent.org/inductees/william-warner#:~:text=Bill%20Warner%20invented%20the%20Avid,in%201987
3. Adrianne Pasquarelli, How DTC brand Titan Casket built a following, *AdAge*, November 18, 2024; https://adage.com/article/special-report-marketers-year/titan-casket-marketers-year-2024/2590631/

Chapter 1

1. National Inventors Hall of Fame, William J. Warner, Digital Nonlinear Editing System, U.S. Patent No. 4,970,663; https://www.invent.org/inductees/william-warner#:~:text=Bill%20Warner%20invented%20the%20Avid,in%201987
2. Frank Beacham, *Broadcast Beat*, "Non-Linear Editing and the Arrival of Avid," 2024, Relevant Media Properties, LLC. https://www.broadcastbeat.com/non-linear-editing-and-the-arrival-of-avid/
3. National Inventors Hall of Fame, William J. Warner, Digital Nonlinear Editing System, U.S. Patent No. 4,970,663; https://www.invent.org/inductees/william-warner#:~:text=Bill%20Warner%20invented%20the%20Avid,in%201987

4. National Inventors Hall of Fame; Visit the NIHF Museum's New Interactive Exhibit, That Seventies Room; https://www.invent.org/blog/innovation-display/NIHF-Museum-Exhibit-That-70s-Room

5. 1989-The Original Avid/1 Demonstration Video; https://www.youtube.com/watch?v=ac1J1bLMucw

6. Variety, Jan. 6, 1999; Avid among 35 to receive Oscars for science, tech; https://variety.com/1999/film/news/avid-among-35-to-receive-oscars-for-science-tech-1117489958/

7. STG News: STG Complete Acquisition of Avid Technology, Press Release, Nov. 7, 2023, Globe Newswire: https://stg.com/news/stg-completes-acquisition-of-avid-technology/

8. Rob Fitzpatrick, "The Mom Test," CreateSpace Independent Publishing Platform (September 10, 2013), Page 11.

9. Tom Ohanian, *Digital Nonlinear Editing, Editing Film and Video on the Desktop*, Focal Press, April 22, 1998. p. 17

10. Clayton Christenson, *Competing Against Luck: The Story of Innovation and Customer Choice*, Harper Business, November 3, 2016.

11. Clayton Christenson, *Competing Against Luck: The Story of Innovation and Customer Choice*, Chapter 2: Progress, Not Products, pp. 24–29, Harper Business, November 3, 2016.

Chapter 2

1. Frank Cespedes and Daniel Weinfurter, *Harvard Business Review* article, "More Universities Need to Teach Sales," April 26, 2016, Brighton, Massachusetts, https://hbr.org/2016/04/more-universities-need-to-teach-sales

2. CNBC, Sports Biz with Darren Rovell, *First Interview with Vince from ShamWow*, Published Tue, Jan 27 2009 5:29 PM EST, Updated Thu, Aug 5 2010 11:35 AM EDT, https://www.cnbc.com/2009/01/27/first-interview-with-vince-from-shamwow.html

3. The ShamWow Commercial (Original, debuted 2007). The Shamwow Guy, posted July 7, 2010, YouTube, https://www.youtube.com/watch?v=1Q39yGLPkMY

4. *Glengarry Glen Ross*, October 2, 1992, produced by New Line Cinema, Zupnik Cinema Group II, and GGR, Inc., directed by Foley, James Foley; based on the play written by Mamet, David.

5. Roberge, M. (2015). *The Sales Acceleration Formula: Using Data, Technology, and Inbound Selling to Go From $0 to $100 Million*. Wiley.

6. Virgin Media O2 Press Release, "Virgin Media O2 and Daisy Group Announce New B2B Company to Create Communications and IT Powerhouse for UK Businesses," May 12, 2025, https://news.virginmediao2

.co.uk/virgin-media-o2-and-daisy-group-announce-new-b2b-company-to-create-communications-and-it-powerhouse-for-uk-businesses/
Virgin Media O2 Press Release, "O2 Daisy Launches, Promising to 'Make Every Business Better' and Shake Up the Telecoms B2B Telecoms Market, Aug. 4, 2025, https://news.virginmediao2.co.uk/o2-daisy-launches-promising-to-make-every-business-better-and-shake-up-the-b2b-telecoms-market/

7. Martin Cave, "The Evolution of Telecommunications Regulation in the UK", *European Economic Review, Volume 41, Issues 3–5,* April 1997, pp. 691–699, https://www.sciencedirect.com/science/article/abs/pii/S0014 292197000305#:~:text=The%20telecommunications%20sector%20 in%20the,increased%20reliance%20on%20standard%20competition

8. Communications Liberalisation in the UK, Key Elements, History & Benefits Department of Trade and Industry, March 2001, https://www.wto.org/english/tratop_e/serv_e/symp_mar02_uk_com_e.pdf

9. Comms Business News section; "Matthew Riley Crowned the UK's Young Entrepreneur of the Year," October 2, 2007, https://www.commsbusiness.co.uk/content/news/matthew-riley-crowned-the-uk-s-young-entrepreneur-of-the-year/

10. *Lancashire Telegraph,* "Businessman's top prize," by the Telegraph Newsdesk, December 13, 2007, https://www.lancashiretelegraph.co.uk/news/1903305.businessmans-top-prize/

11. Peter Campbell for *The Daily Mail,* as appears in *This is Money*: "CITY INTERVIEW: Working as Apprentice judge put me off showbusiness for life, says Daisy founder Matthew Riley," Sept. 4, 2014, https://www.thisismoney.co.uk/money/markets/article-2742592/CITY-INTERVIEW-Telecoms-entrepreneur-Matthew-Riley-upwards-trajectory.html

12. Patrick Killeen *Business Cloud* article, "Daisy Sounder Says Virgin Media O2 is His Biggest Deal Yet"; May 12, 2025, https://businesscloud.co.uk/news/daisy-founder-says-virgin-media-o2-deal-is-his-biggest-yet/

13. Paul Lipscombe, *Data Center Dynamics,* "Media O2 Business and Daisy Group to create B2B telecoms group in UK," May 13, 2025, https://www.datacenterdynamics.com/en/news/virgin-media-o2-business-and-daisy-group-to-create-b2b-telecoms-group-in-uk/

14. Matthew Ramirez; Pitchgrade, BT Group PLC: Business Model, SWOT analytics, and Competitors, January 20, 2024, https://pitchgrade.com/companies/bt-group-plc

15. The Largest Language Service Providers: 2023; CSA Research, North Chelmsford, MA, https://csa-research.com/Featured-Content/For-LSPs/Global-Market-Study/TOP-100-LSPs-2023

16. TransPerfect Press Release, "TransPerfect Billed Revenues Increase 3% in 2024 to $1.23 Billion," April 10, 2025, https://www.transperfect.com/about/press/transperfect-billed-revenues-increase-3-2024-123-billion

17. Forbes, 2025 America's Richest Self-Made Women Net Worth, Profile: Liz Elting, #78, $458M as of 6/3/25, https://www.forbes.com/profile/liz-elting/

18. Elting, L. (2023). *Dream Big and Win: Translating Passion into Purpose and Creating a Billion Dollar Business.* Wiley.

19. Elting, L. (2023). *Dream Big and Win, Translating Passion into Purpose, and Creating a Billion Dollar Business,* 46. Wiley.

20. Marisa Guthrie; "How the '*Today*' Show remained Number 1 for 15 years, *The Hollywood Reporter,* December 11, 2010, https://www.hollywoodreporter.com/tv/tv-news/today-show-remained-no-1-58976/

21. Couric, K. (2012). *The Best Advice I Ever Got: Lessons from Extraordinary Lives.* Random House Publishing.

22. Couric, K. memoir (2021). *Going There.* Little Brown and Company.

23. N. Louis Shipley, and William R. Kerr, "Katie Couic Media: Landing the First Client" case study, revised, March, 2022, Harvard Business School Publishing (page 02)

24. 2010 duPont-Columbia University Award Winners, "The Sarah Palin Interviews", CBS News & Katie Couric, July 14, 2010, https://dupont.org/2010winners

25. George Foster Peabody Award, Personal Award: Katie Couric for "Confronting Colon Cancer", 2001

26. CBS News, "CBS News Wins Murrow Awards," For the second year in a row, the CBS Evening News with Katie Couric won for the best newscast, which aired November 12, 2008, https://www.cbsnews.com/news/cbs-news-wins-murrow-awards/

27. *AdWeek*, "Katie Couric Wins Award Named for Her Predecessor," March 10, 2009, https://www.adweek.com/tvnewser/katie-couric-wins-award-named-for-her-evening-news-predecessor/

28. *Time Magazine*, The 2010 TIME 100, TIME 100 Alumnae: Katie Couric, https://content.time.com/time/specials/packages/article/0,28804,1984685_1985123_1985121,00.html

29. Jordan Riefe, *The Hollywood Reporter*, "Stars Turn Out for Katie Couric's Under the Gun Premiere in Beverly Hills," May 4, 2016, https://www.hollywoodreporter.com/movies/movie-news/stars-turn-katie-courics-890561/

30. Claudia Puig, *USA Today*, "Katie Couric is 'Fed Up' with Childhood Obesity," January 29, 2014, https://www.usatoday.com/story/life/movies/2014/01/29/katie-couric-documentary/5019841/

31. N. Louis Shipley and William R. Kerr, Katie Couric Media: Landing the First Client, case study, revised March, 2022, Harvard Business School Publishing (page 02)

32. Glamour, 30 Years of WOTY: Unforgettable Moments from Every *Glamour* Women of the Year Awards; Katie Couric, 1992, 2002, 2006 Woman of the Year, https://www.glamour.com/story/women-of-the-year-history

33. N. Louis Shipley, and William R. Kerr, Katie Couric Media: Landing the First Client, case study, revised March, 2022, Harvard Business School Publishing

34. Mark Leslie, and Charles A. Holloway, "The Sales Learning Curve," Harvard Business Review" magazine, July-August 2006 issue, https://hbr.org/2006/07/the-sales-learning-curve

35. BANT, is a sales qualification method and stands for Budget, Authority, Need and Timing. First invented by IBM in the 1950s. Sandler Method

36. The Sandler Selling System, https://sandler.com/sandler-selling-system/?utm_source=googleads&utm_medium=paid&utm_campaign=sandlerbrand&utm_content=rsa_2&utm_term=sandler%20sales%20methodology&utm_campaign=Sandler+Brand&utm_source=adwords&utm_medium=ppc&hsa_acc=5666182706&hsa_cam=20085246449&hsa_grp=151573391969&hsa_ad=666561971997&hsa_src=g&hsa_tgt=kwd-1337047301726&hsa_kw=sandler%20sales%20methodology&hsa_mt=p&hsa_net=adwords&hsa_ver=3&gad_source=1&gad_campaignid=20085246449&gbraid=0AAAAADtN61g0t84IMgmNsRV-JTGHbXfY8&gclid=CjwKCAjwx8nCBhAwEiwA_z__02v84DIJ-KJyLS6koaWyFgqSS66qsMA1FpGkhObFEVg_UmvI_IyOHhoC2-wQAvD_BwE

37. Meddic Sales Methodology, https://meddicc.com/meddpicc-sales-methodology-and-process

38. Rackham, N. (1988). *Spin Selling: The Best Validated Sales Method Available Today. Developed From Research Studies of 35,000 Sales Calls. Used By the Top Sales Forces Across the World.* McGraw-Hill.

39. Dickson, M. and Adamson, B. (2011). *The Challenger Sale: Taking Control of the Customer Conversation.* Portfolio/Penguin.

40. Evan Andrews, History.com Who Invented Beer? https://www.history.com/articles/who-invented-beer

Chapter 3

1. US Small Business Administration, SBA-guaranteed business loans, https://www.sba.gov/

2. *Eagle-Tribune:* Best of the Eagle-Tribune 2024, Oct. 30, 2024, Starts on p. 4; https://www.eagletribune.com/special_sections/best-of-the-eagle-tribune-2024/pdf_63c82c7c-9568-11ef-a013-2bf423983783.html
Eagle-Tribune: Best of the Eagle-Tribune 2023, Oct. 28, 2023 pp. S8 & S9: https://www.eagletribune.com/special_sections/best-of-eagle-tribune-2023/pdf_759e9420-73fb-11ee-bff4-a7f0ba3f8b36.html

Eagle-Tribune: Best of the Eagle-Tribune 2022, Oct. 30, 2022 pp. S8 & S9. https://www.eagletribune.com/special_sections/et-best-2022/pdf_2a48dbc4-55e4-11ed-b4ac-1b166d10256f.html

3. The Economist, The Bright New Age of Venture Capital, Nov. 25, 2021, https://www.economist.com/finance-and-economics/2021/11/23/the-bright-new-age-of-venture-capital/21806438

4. Taibbi, R. (2023). Why So Many Marriages End After Eight Years: Statistics Show That Most Couples Divorce After Eight Years. *Psychology Today*. https://www.psychologytoday.com/us/blog/fixing-families/202304/why-so-many-marriages-end-after-8-years.

5. National Center for Charitable Statistics, https://urbaninstitute.github.io/nccs/

6. Candid: US Social Sector, Organizations. There are 1,935,344 registered nonprofits in the United States, 2025, https://candid.org/explore-issues/us-social-sector/organizations

7. National Council of Nonprofits, Running a Nonprofit, Financial Transparency and Public Disclosure Requirements, 2025, https://www.councilofnonprofits.org/running-nonprofit/ethics-accountability/financial-transparency-and-public-disclosure-requirements#:~:text=Tax%2Dexempt%20nonprofits%20are%20required,IRS%20related%20to%20the%20application).

8. Jackson, K.T. (ed.) (1995). *The Encyclopedia of New York City*, 673. New Haven: Yale University Press ISBN 0300055366.

9. Eisenstadt, P. (2011). *Rochdale Village: Robert Moses, 6,000 Families, and New York City's Great Experiment in Integrated Housing*, 49–52. Cornell University Press ISBN 978-0-8014-5968-9. Retrieved April 2, 2016.
   Sam Roberts, "Before Public Housing, a City Life Cleared Away," *The New York Times*, May 8, 2005, Retrieved April 2, 2016.

10. Edward C. Burkes, "'Social Profile' of Depressed South Jamaica," *The New York Times*, April 30, 1972, section A, p. 14.

11. Peter Eisenstadt, "Rochdale Village and the rise and fall of integrated housing in New York City", nyc.gov, 2007

12. Peter Kerr, "A Crack Plague in Queens Bring Violence and Fear," *The New York Times*, October 19, 1987, section A, p. 1

13. Tabor Academy, Community Recognition, Paul B. Fireman '62, https://www.taboracademy.org/alumni/alumni-recognition

14. Tabor Today Alumni Magazine, "Celebrating Distinguished Alums," https://www.taboracademy.org/magazine/details/~board/alumni-magazine/post/celebrating-distinguished-tabor-alums

15. https://genius.com/A-tribe-called-quest-8-million-stories-lyrics

16. Susan Cohen, Benjamin Hallen and Christopher Bingham, "What Sets Successful Start-up Accelerators Apart," *Harvard Business Review*, March 12, 2024

Chapter 4

1. US Hockey Hall of Fame, Mark Fusco bio, https://www.ushockeyhall offame.com/page/show/831070-mark-fusco

2. Hobey Baker, Character Builds Excellence, Mark Fusco, https://hobeybaker.com/hbma/mark-fusco/

3. Deloitte Press Release, Deloitte: "85% of Women Surveyed Who Played Sports Say It's Important to Their Career Success", September 19, 2023. The online survey of 1,100 currently and previously employed Americans, age 18+, was conducted in August 2023. For more details on our survey please visit: https://www2.deloitte.com/us/en/pages/about-deloitte/articles/supporting-professional-women-everywhere.html. https://www2.deloitte.com/us/en/pages/about-deloitte/articles/press-releases/new-deloitte-tv-spots-turn-the-tables-on-fandom-as-survey-reveals-girls-who-play-sports-are-likely-to-have-successful-careers.html

4. "A Tribute to Larry Evans: History of Aspen Technology from the Aspen Project to the Year 2000" https://cache.org/sites/default/files/winter15-Evans-tribute.pdf, slides 24, 28, 30, 33 and 37.

5. Thomas M. Huber, "Introduction to Lesson 5," US Army Command and General Staff College, C610 Term I Syllabus/Book of Readings (Fort Leavenworth:USACGSC, August 1996), p. 134 (hereafter cited as Huber, Lesson 5)

6. New Histories, "Corps and Columns–The Battle Tactics of Napoleon Bonaparte and Why They Failed Him at Waterloo," Volume 6 I Issue 1 - War and Peace; https://newhistories.sites.sheffield.ac.uk/volumes/2014-15/volume-6/issue-1-war-and-peace/corps-and-columns-the-battle-tactics-of-napoleon-bonaparte-and-why-they-f

7. History Extra, "Napoleon Bonaparte's Greatest Triumphs and Disasters," https://www.historyextra.com/period/georgian/napoleon-greatest-battle-triumph-disaster-victory-defeat/

8. *The Personal Memoirs of US Grant*, Vintage Bookworks, 2024, page 396. Originally published in two volumes by Charles L. Webster and Company, 1886.

9. "Why Distributed Leadership is the Future of Management", by Meredith Summers, *Ideas Made To Matter* I Leadership section I MIT Sloan School of Management, April 19, 2022, https://mitsloan.mit.edu/ideas-made-to-matter/why-distributed-leadership-future-management

10. Peter Kelly, Sara Heston, *2024 Search Fund Study* Research Overview, Stanford Graduate School of Business, CASE E-870 JUNE 28, 2024, Page 7, https://www.gsb.stanford.edu/faculty-research/case-studies/2024-search-fund-study

11. US Navy Cyclopedia, "The Phases of SEAL Training," https://usnavy.com/navy-seal-training-program/

12. U.S. Department of Labor, Veterans' Employment and Training Services, HIRE Vets Medallion Program, https://www.dol.gov/agencies/vets/programs/hvmp

13. *Swedish Forest Industries*, Facts & Figures, Sweden's Forest Industry In Brief, December 5, 2024, https://www.forestindustries.se/forest-industry/statistics/facts-and-figures/

14. Swedish Wood, The forest and sustainable forestry Forest to spare, Publisher: Anna Ryberg Ågren, 2025, https://www.swedishwood.com/wood-facts/about-wood/wood-and-sustainability/the-forest-and-sustainable-forestry/

15. Tomas Ekbom, Task 39 May 2016 NewsletterAdvanced BiofuelsUSA, "Sweden Takes the Lead in Biofuel-Use in Europe," https://advanced biofuelsusa.info/sweden-takes-the-lead-in-biofuel-use-in-europe

Chapter 5

1. Phillips, Brad The Media Training Bible:101 Things you Absolutely Positively Need to Know Before Your Next Interview, SpeakGood Press, January 16, 2013.

2. Phillips, Brad The Media Training Bible:101 Things you Absolutely Positively Need to Know Before Your Next Interview, p. 38, SpeakGood Press, January 16, 2013.

3. Phillips, Brad The Media Training Bible:101 Things you Absolutely Positively Need to Know Before Your Next Interview, p. 40, SpeakGood Press, January 16, 2013.

4. Phillips, Brad The Media Training Bible:101 Things you Absolutely Positively Need to Know Before Your Next Interview, pp. 64 & 65, SpeakGood Press, January 16, 2013.

5. Who Invented Pizza - The History of 'Za, Streets of New York, April 30, 2021.

6. Pizza a Portafoglio (Wallet Pizza) in Naples: What is It, It's History and Where to Eat It, Cookist.com, https://www.cookist.com/pizza-a-portafoglio-wallet-pizza-in-naples-what-is-it-its-history-and-where-to-eat-it/

7. Statistics, National Funeral Directors Association (NFDA), 2023, https://nfda.org/news/statistics#:~:text=%247%2C848,click%20here%20to%20learn%20more.

8. Funeral Costs and Pricing Checklist, Federal Trade Commission, Consumer Advice, July 2012, https://consumer.ftc.gov/articles/funeral-costs-pricing-checklist#:~:text=A%20casket%20often%20is%20the,primarily%20for%20their%20visual%20appeal

9. Coffin & Casket Manufacturing in the US - Number of Businesses (2005–2031), NAICS OD5365 Last Updated: June 2025, https://www .ibisworld.com/united-states/number-of-businesses/coffin-casket-manufacturing/5365/

10. Pasquarelli, Adrianne, How DTC brand Titan Casket built a following, AdAge, November 18, 2024, https://adage.com/article/special-report-marketers-year/titan-casket-marketers-year-2024/2590631/

11. The FTC Funeral Rule, Federal Trade Commission, Consumer Advice, July, 2012, https://consumer.ftc.gov/articles/ftc-funeral-rule#:~:text= The%20Funeral%20Rule%20gives%20you,items%20you%20do%20 not%20want

12. Sarah Marsden-Ille, The US Funeral Industry Today, November 25, 2024, https://www.us-funerals.com/the-us-funeral-industry-today/

13. Buell, Spencer, The Boston Globe, "Methuen's Titan Casket makes a cameo in Taylor Swift's 'Anti-Hero' music video: The budget casket company has emerged as a go-to for the entertainment industry in recent years," October 26, 2022, https://www.bostonglobe.com/2022/10/26/ metro/methuens-titan-casket-makes-cameo-taylor-swifts-anti-hero-music-video/

14. Marques Brownlee, MKBHD, 20.1M subscribers, July 2, 2025, YouTube. https://www.youtube.com/user/marquesbrownlee

15. Marques Keith Brownlee, MKBHD, November 23, 2022, Youtube. https://www.youtube.com/watch?v=mv9afG2Dm9I

16. Connecting Directors, "Genius Marketing! Titan Casket's & Dastmalcian Have Done It Again with Grave Conversations," May 1, 2024, https:// connectingdirectors.com/68143-titan-casket-launches-grave-conversations

17. Aaron Couch, Why Stars are Giving Interviews While Lying in Caskets, The Hollywood Reporter, March 28, 2025, https://www.hollywood reporter.com/movies/movie-news/grave-conversations-david-dastmalchian-1236175218/

18. Nelson, Samantha, Adweek, "Titan Casket and Maximum Effort Want to 'Bury Daylight Savings' in Darkly Comic Ad," March 8, 2024, https:// www.adweek.com/creativity/titan-casket-and-maximum-effort-want-to-bury-daylight-savings-in-darkly-comic-ad/

19. Adrianne Pasquarelli, Adage.com, "Marketers of the Year: How DTC brand Titan Casket built a following," November 18, 2024, https://adage .com/article/special-report-marketers-year/titan-casket-marketers-year-2024/2590631/

Chapter 6

1. Founder Forum Group, The Ultimate Start-up Guide with Statistics (2024–2025), May 9, 2025.

2. Feeding America. "Fighting food waste and hunger through food rescue," https://www.feedingamerica.org/our-work/reduce-food-waste#:~:text=In%20the%20United%20States%2C%20people,all%20the%20food%20in%20America

3. MassChallenge, "Start-ups win big at the 2015 MassChallenge," October 29, 2015, https://masschallenge.org/articles/start-ups-win-big-2015-masschallenge-boston-awards-ceremony/

4. Danielle Gould, "How Spoiler Alert is Growing Its Food Waste Marketplace," Food+Tech Connect, March 27, 2017, https://foodtech connect.com/2017/03/27/how-spoiler-alert-is-growing-its-food-waste-marketplace/

5. Tracxn, Spoiler Alert - Company Profile, June 24, 2025, https://tracxn .com/d/companies/spoiler-alert/__8Wkq0Y7fMHRQ3Z0kSLPrLDyc3 5j88WdaCPzgBB8fjIw

6. Forbes, 30 Under 30–Social Entrepreneurs, Ricky Ashenfelder, Cofounder, Spoiler Alert, Boston, MA, 2017, https://www.forbes.com/ profile/ricky-ashenfelter/

7. Janelle Nanos, *The Boston Globe*, "Spoiler Alert: It makes sure nothing goes to waste," November 27, 2016, https://www.bostonglobe.com/business/ 2016/11/27/platform-helps-rescue-food-before-spoils-get-needy/ NebFcir4xf8YPVWMKbUyQK/story.html

8. Jillian Kwong and Keri Pearlson; *ScholarSpace*, "Supply Chain Cybersecurity and Small and Medium-Sized Enterprises (SMEs): Exploring Shortcomings in Third Party Risk Management of SMEs" January 3, 2024, https://scholarspace.manoa.hawaii.edu/items/993cbf7f-45b8-456f-b707-a84cbdec8a56

9. Palatty, Nivedita James; Astra, Security Audit, 51 Small Business Cyber Attack Statistics 2025 (and What We Can Do About Them), June 16, 2025, https://www.getastra.com/blog/security-audit/small-business-cyber-attack-statistics/

10. Bias, Daniel and Ljungqvist, Alexander "Great Recession Babies: How Are Start-ups Shaped By Macro Conditions At Birth?" Swedish House of Finance Research Paper No. 23-01, Posted on SSNR December 22, 2022; Paper last revised: May 26, 2024; https://papers.ssrn.com/sol3/ papers.cfm?abstract_id=4298934

11. Seggie, Steven H.; Talay, Berk; and Pauwels, Koen MIT Sloan Management Review, *When Launching a Product During a Recession Pays Off*, April 29, 2025; Magazine, Summer 2025 Issue; https://sloanreview .mit.edu/article/when-launching-a-product-during-a-recession-pays-off/#:~:text=We%20found%20that%2C%20on%20average,recession %20is%20better%20than%20earlier.

12. Matt Rosoff, *Business Insider*, "BORN FROM THE ASHES: Big Tech Companies Founded During Busts and Receissions," August 16, 2011, https://www.businessinsider.com/great-tech-companies-that-started-in-terrible-economic-times-2011-8

13. Reuters, by Reuters, *Explainer: How four big companies control the U.S. beef industry*, June 17, 2021, https://www.reuters.com/business/how-four-big-companies-control-us-beef-industry-2021-06-17/
14. N. Louis Shipley, Patricia Favreau, and Mel Martin, "Seemore Meats & Veggies," Harvard Business School Case Study, February 10, 2023, p. 4.
15. N. Louis Shipley, Patricia Favreau, and Mel Martin, "Seemore Meats & Veggies," Harvard Business School Case Study, February 10, 2023, p. 4.
16. N. Louis Shipley, Patricia Favreau, and Mel Martin, "Seemore Meats & Veggies," Harvard Business School Case Study, February 10, 2023, p. 4.
17. Good Food Institute (GFI), Investing in Alternative Protein, 2025, https://gfi.org/investment/
18. N. Louis Shipley, Patricia Favreau, and Mel Martin, "Seemore Meats & Veggies," Harvard Business School Case Study, February 10, 2023, p. 4.
19. N. Louis Shipley, Patricia Favreau, and Mel Martin, "Seemore Meats & Veggies," Harvard Business School Case Study, February 10, 2023, p. 6.

Chapter 7

1. Azoulay, P., Jones, B.F., Kim, J.D., and Miranda, J. (2020). Age and High-Growth Entrepreneurship. *American Economic Review: Insights 2* (1): 65–82. American Economic Association, https://www.aeaweb.org/articles?id=10.1257/aeri.20180582.
2. Pierre Azoulay, Benjamin F. Jones, J. Daniel Kim, Javier Miranda, "Research: The Average Age of a Successful Startup Founder Is 45," *Harvard Business Review*, July 11, 2018, https://hbr.org/2018/07/research-the-average-age-of-a-successful-startup-founder-is-45
3. Brian Stelter, MSNBC.com May Change Its Name, *New York Times*, October 6, 2010, https://www.nytimes.com/2010/10/07/business/media/07msnbc.html?searchResultPosition=6
4. Somers, Meredith, "Intrapreneurship, Explained," *Ideas Made To Matter*, MIT Sloan School of Management, July 21, 2018, https://mitsloan.mit.edu/ideas-made-to-matter/intrapreneurship-explained
5. The Factal Story, Factal Blog, "Most startup stories begin with an idea," https://blog.factal.com/the-factal-story/#:~:text=Breaking%20News%20grew%20into%20a,phenomenon%20in%20the%20news%20space.
6. BBC News, "Nice attack: At least 84 killed by lorry at Bastille Day celebrations," July 15, 2016
7. Bob Brennan Elected Chief Executive Officer of Iron Mountain, June 5, 2008, Company Website, https://investors.ironmountain.com/news/news-details/2008/Bob-Brennan-Elected-Chief-Executive-Officer-of-Iron-Mountain/default.aspx
8. Elting, Liz; LizElting.com, About Liz, https://lizelting.com/aboutMazu Netowrks, Dennis Hoffman, Storigen Systens, Mark Overington, Digital Media On Demand Matt Danilowicz, INews, Clear-Com, Vitec Group.

Index